BY SCRIPTURE
ALONE THROUGH
FAITH ALONE
BY GRACE
ALONE THROUGH
CHRIST ALONE
GLORY
GOD ALONE

TO GOD ALONE

5 CORE BELIEFS OF THE REFORMATION

BRANDON D. SMITH

TGC THE GOSPEL COALITION

LifeWay Press® Nashville, Tennessee

Printed by LifeWay Press® • © 2017 The Gospel Coalition

Requests for permission should be addressed in writing to
LifeWay Press, One LifeWay Plaza,
Nashville, TN 37234-0144.

ISBN: 978-1-4300-6464-0
Item 005791921

Dewey Decimal Classification: 248.84
Subject Heading: REFORMATION \ CHRISTIAN LIFE \ DISCIPLESHIP

Printed in the United States of America

Student Ministry Publishing
LifeWay Resources
One LifeWay Plaza
Nashville, TN 37234-0144

We believe that the Bible has God for its author; salvation for its end; and truth, without any mixture of error, for its matter and that all Scripture is totally true and trustworthy. To review LifeWay's doctrinal guideline, please visit www.lifeway.com/doctrinalguideline.

CONTENTS

ABOUT THE GOSPEL COALITION

THE GOSPEL COALITION is a fellowship of evangelical churches deeply committed to renewing our faith in the gospel of Christ and to reforming our ministry practices to conform fully to the Scriptures. We have become deeply concerned about some movements within traditional evangelicalism that seem to be diminishing the church's life and leading us away from our historic beliefs and practices. On the one hand, we're troubled by the idolatry of personal consumerism and the politicization of faith; on the other hand, we're distressed by the unchallenged acceptance of theological and moral relativism. These movements have led to the easy abandonment of both biblical truth and the transformed living mandated by our historic faith. We not only hear of these influences but also see their effects. We've committed ourselves to invigorating churches with new hope and compelling joy, based on the promises received by grace alone through faith alone in Christ alone.

We believe that in many evangelical churches a deep and broad consensus exists about the truths of the gospel. Yet we often see the celebration of our union with Christ replaced by the age-old attractions of power and affluence or by monastic retreats into ritual, liturgy, and sacrament. Any replacement for the gospel will never promote a missionhearted faith anchored in enduring truth that works itself out in unashamed discipleship eager to stand the tests of Kingdom calling and sacrifice. We desire to advance along the King's highway, always aiming to provide gospel advocacy, encouragement, and education so that current and next-generation church leaders are better equipped to fuel their ministries with principles and practices that glorify the Savior and do good to those for whom He shed His life's blood.

We want to generate a unified effort among all peoples—an effort that's zealous to honor Christ and multiply His disciples, joining in a true coalition for Jesus. Such a biblically grounded and united mission is the only enduring future for the church. This reality compels us to stand with others who are stirred by the conviction that the mercy of God in Jesus Christ is our only hope of eternal salvation. We desire to champion this gospel with clarity, compassion, courage, and joy, gladly linking hearts with fellow believers across denominational, ethnic, and class lines.

Our desire is to serve the church we love by inviting all our brothers and sisters to join us in an effort to renew the contemporary church in the ancient gospel of Christ so that we truly speak and live for Him in a way that clearly communicates to our age. As pastors, we intend to do this in our churches through the usual means of His grace: prayer, ministry of the Word, baptism and the Lord's Supper, and the fellowship of the saints. We yearn to work with all who seek the lordship of Christ over the whole of life with unabashed hope in the power of the Holy Spirit to transform individuals, communities, and cultures.

ABOUT THE AUTHOR

 BRANDON D. SMITH works with the Christian Standard Bible at LifeWay Christian Resources and teaches theology at various schools. The author of *Rooted: Theology for Growing Christians* and *They Spoke of Me: How Jesus Unlocks the Old Testament*, Brandon also cohosts the *Word Matters* podcast. He holds a BA in biblical studies from Dallas Baptist University and an MA in systematic and historical theology from Criswell College. He is pursuing a PhD in theology at Ridley College in Melbourne, Australia. Brandon lives near Nashville, Tennessee, with his wife, Christa, and their two daughters, Harper and Emma.

HOW TO USE

This Bible study provides a guided process for individuals and small groups to explore the five *alone* statements that came out of the Reformation and to discover the practical implications of those statements for believers today. This study is divided into those five statements, along with an introductory week that will provide a good foundation for understanding these Reformation tenets. Here are the topics you and your group will examine together:

1. **WHY THE REFORMATION MATTERS**
2. **SCRIPTURE ALONE**
3. **GRACE ALONE**
4. **FAITH ALONE**
5. **CHRIST ALONE**
6. **GLORY TO GOD ALONE**

One week of Bible study is devoted to each of these topics, and each week is divided into four sections:

1. **START**
2. **THE BIG IDEA**
3. **GOSPEL APPLICATION**
4. **DIGGING DEEPER**

In these sections you'll find biblical teaching, interactive questions, and personal studies that will help you understand and apply the teaching.

In addition, a Leader Guide is provided to help you spark gospel conversations. Each Leader Guide session is divided into four sections:

1. **GETTING STARTED** focuses participants on the topic of the session.
2. **HIGHLIGHTS** provides additional facts and information about the Reformation.
3. **TAKE ACTION** guides the group to respond to and apply what they've learned.
4. **BEFORE YOU GO** is a quick reminder of what students need to do before the next group meeting.

WHY THE REFORMATION MATTERS

Let's test your American history knowledge. Match the dates in the left-hand column with the corresponding event on the right side.

1492	Boston Tea Party
1607	The First Great Awakening
1620	Christopher Columbus discovered America
1636	The Declaration of Independence
1732	Benjamin Franklin's famous kite experiment
1752	The settlement of Jamestown
1773	Establishment of Plymouth Colony
1776	Harvard College founded
1783	The end of the American Revolutionary War

Whether you missed a few or got them all right, we need to know that history is more than key dates associated with important figures and events from the past. While there are certainly historical moments we must cover, the subject of history is more than moments, especially for Christians.

The Christian faith is a historical faith. It has its roots in Old Testament events and promises, and peaks in the life, death, and resurrection of Jesus of Nazareth. In fact, history is so much a part of our faith that Paul said that if Jesus hadn't been raised from the dead, then our faith is worthless and we are still in our sins (1 Cor. 15:12-19). In other words, faith isn't opposite of real events or reasons or evidences, but stands on the historical reality that Jesus Christ rose from the dead.

This study is unique for several reasons. In the first place, it is a study that covers one of history's most significant time periods—the Reformation, which took place 500 years ago. But this study will also take you on a journey through some of the major Christian convictions that came from the Reformation. In the words of church historian Justo L. Gonzalez, "Without understanding that past, we are unable to understand ourselves, for in a sense the past still lives in us and influences who we are and how we understand the Christian message."[1] Christians should always be students of history, not only for the obvious fact that it is His story that we are exploring, but also for the simple reality that there is much to be gained on a personal and devotional level by learning from the heroes of the faith who have gone before us.

THE BIG IDEA

The time for silence is past, and the time to speak has come. —Martin Luther[2]

To set the scene for the Reformation, imagine a young, newly ordained Catholic priest standing in front of the church, ready to officiate his first mass. These priests were expected to have clean hearts before officiating—no sin unconfessed.

But as Martin Luther began to recite the introductory portion of the mass, with the bread and wine on the altar in front of him, he almost passed out. "I was utterly stupefied and terror-stricken. … Who am I, that I should lift up mine eyes or raise my hands to the divine Majesty?"[3]

Luther's fear was not misplaced. He knew he was a sinner, and he couldn't live up to the cleanliness required of a Catholic priest. Who could?

Read Proverbs 3:5-6. Have you ever experienced a moment when you weren't sure if God approved of your decision? How did you respond?

Looking back, in what ways was God faithful in that moment, even in your uncertainty?

THE ACCIDENTAL REFORMATION?

On October 31, 1517—a decade after his ordination as a priest—Luther nailed his now-famous 95 Theses to the door of the All Saints' Church in Wittenberg, Germany. Of all these 95 affirmations and concerns, the main point was simple: You can't buy God's grace and there is no authority higher than the Bible. The Church missed this, and that's a dangerous place to be.

If you were in Luther's situation, how would you have handled it?

Read 1 Peter 3:13-17. Circle where you are on the line below when it comes to defending your faith.

Terrified	Not Confident	Willing	Ready and Able

Luther wasn't spreading his theses around on little gospel tracts. He wasn't shouting his complaints from rooftops or using some medieval form of social media to tell his friends how angry he was. When he nailed his letter to the church's door, he invited debate in a way that was common for his time.[4] He wanted to hash out the truths of the Bible with others. He wanted truth to reign. If others were right, Luther thought, they'd demonstrate it by proving him wrong.

By 1518, his controversial writings began to pick up steam. And in 1521, Luther appeared on trial at the Diet of Worms (this had nothing to do with eating worms, by the way. Worms was a town in Germany, and a diet was an assembly held by the leaders of the Holy Roman Empire). At Worms, Luther was asked to defend himself. His response summed up the Reformation:

> I am bound by the Scriptures I have quoted and my conscience is captive to the Word of God. I cannot and will not recant anything, since it is neither safe nor right to go against conscience.[5]

THE CLOUD OF WITNESSES

Of course, the Reformation didn't end when Martin Luther died in 1546. Its impact is still felt today. Most obviously, if you're any sort of Protestant (not Roman Catholic or Eastern Orthodox), you're a product of the Reformation. We stand on the shoulders of Christians in the past, and knowing where we came from will help us keep moving forward.

> Therefore, since we are surrounded by so great a cloud of witnesses, let us also lay aside every weight, and sin which clings so closely, and let us run with endurance the race that is set before us, looking to Jesus, the founder and perfecter of our faith, who for the joy that was set before him endured the cross, despising the shame, and is seated at the right hand of the throne of God. —*Hebrews 12:1-2*

These "witnesses" are those listed in Hebrews 11. They are people who came before us, who experienced both peace and suffering for their faith. The writer of Hebrews wanted readers to understand that those who came before us laid a foundation that still matters today.

Let's look at some of these witnesses in Hebrews 11:

- Abel's faithfulness to God was a "more acceptable sacrifice" than his brother, Cain's. Abel offered the acceptable blood sacrifice while Cain merely offered fruit. Cain eventually became the world's first murderer, killing Abel out of jealous rage. Yet Hebrews declares about Abel, "through his faith, though [Abel] died, he still speaks" (Heb. 11:4). His sacrifice for God—which ended up costing him his life—is an example to us today.

- Noah was commanded by God to build an ark. He didn't fully know why, and his neighbors mocked him. But even in their mocking, Noah was faithful to God's command, being motivated by "reverent fear" (Heb. 11:7). His desire to follow God was more important than his own ego.

- Abraham was willing to lay his own son, Isaac, on the altar and sacrifice him (sound familiar?) to follow God's commands. God spared Isaac's life because, as the writer of Hebrews writer said, "He considered that God was able even to raise him from the dead, from which, figuratively speaking, he did receive him back" (Heb. 11:19). Abraham's faith was so strong, not even the death of his son would shake his faith that God was powerful and good.

Name one person who has greatly influenced you. Why did they have such an impact on you?

Jot down the name of one person you can influence for the gospel. How can you intentionally begin to reach that person?

TRUTH IN A WORLD OF OPPOSITION

It's common today to hear things like, "How can we know what truth really is?" and "How dare you tell me that your truth is better than my truth!" The world often accuses anyone with strong convictions of being intolerant, hateful, and exclusive.

In Acts 5, the apostles taught about Jesus in the temple courts right after being released from prison for doing just that. They ran into trouble with the authorities again, and were arrested and brought before the religious leaders. When told never to preach again, they argued that doing so would be disobedience to God. They were beaten, released, and warned not to preach the gospel again. Their response? Let's take a look:

Then they left the presence of the council, rejoicing that they were counted worthy to suffer dishonor for the name. And every day, in the temple and from house to house, they did not cease teaching and preaching that the Christ is Jesus. —*Acts 5:41-42*

Read Acts 5:21-42. Notice that the apostles were not angry or hostile, even though they didn't shy away from their convictions. Why did they remain calm?

Think of an example from your own life when you faced opposition in some way for your faith. How did you respond?

How does the gospel make us hopeful even in the face of opposition and difficulties?

BELIEF IN ACTION

Even though we may not seek out opposition to our faith, we do have to realize that the faith of the apostles, the Reformers, and everyone in between is the same faith we have today. They weren't super Christians who had a more godly calling than ours. God used them to reform their times, and God can use us to reform ours today.

The first step for us is to know what we believe and why we believe it. That's why those who came before us were willing to do anything and go anywhere for the mission of God. They realized belief and action can't be separated. You act on what you believe.

How did you feel about church history before reading this section?
A. I hadn't thought much about it.
B. I thought it was interesting, but not overly important to my life.
C. Christians from church history were inspirations to my faith.

How has learning some of the history behind the Reformation changed how you view what you believe?

List three takeaways from Martin Luther's life and the story of the Reformation.

THE SOLAS

We should not investigate what the Lord has left hidden in secret ... nor neglect what he has brought out into the open, so that we may not be convicted of excessive curiosity on the one hand, or of excessive ingratitude on the other. —*John Calvin*[6]

The core truths of the Reformation may be summarized in five *solas*. The word *sola* is the Latin word for *alone* or *only*. The five are: *sola scriptura* (by Scripture alone), *sola gratia* (by grace alone), *sola fide* (through faith alone), *solus Christus* (through Christ alone), and *Soli Deo gloria* (glory to God alone).

These were not terms coined by Luther or any of the Reformers, though Reformers used them in varying ways. Instead, they have more recently become the way to describe the DNA of the Reformation. As we'll see, they're more than just a bunch of cold Latin terms that academics throw around in church history books. The five solas, like the Reformation itself, are incredibly practical. They are grounded in real life, in the day-to-day aspects of following Jesus. They're the most important, basic truths you can ever believe.

But God, being rich in mercy, because of the great love with which he loved us, even when we were dead in our trespasses, made us alive together with Christ—by grace you have been saved. —*Ephesians 2:4-5*

Look at the five *solas* again. How does Ephesians 2:4-5 give an overview of the truth behind them?

Which describes you most?
[ ] I know more facts about the Bible than I actually live out day to day.
[ ] I'm all about action, but can't always articulate what I believe.

GOSPEL APPLICATION

Let's finish this session by taking a quick glance at the *Solas*.

SOLA SCRIPTURA—SCRIPTURE ALONE

All Scripture is breathed out by God and profitable for teaching, for reproof, for correction, and for training in righteousness, that the man of God may be complete, equipped for every good work. —*2 Timothy 3:16-17*

The Church in Luther's day didn't mesh well with this Scripture. Roman Catholicism taught that the Pope held equal authority to the Scriptures. In a sense, they believed the Pope had as much power as Scripture.

But Paul told Timothy that Scripture is from God and makes Christians "complete." It's not Scripture *plus* the Pope or Scripture *plus* anything else.

Why can no person—not the Pope or your pastor or your best friend—hold the same authority as God's Word?

SOLA GRATIA—GRACE ALONE

For sin will have no dominion over you, since you are not under law but under grace. —*Romans 6:14*

Grace is most easily defined as undeserved favor. God gives grace because He's loving and merciful, not because we deserve it. It's free. Absolutely free. We are saved by grace alone.

The church can't sell grace, and Luther knew this. Indulgences worked similar to "get out of jail free" cards in Monopoly—you pay a sum to the church, and leaders grant grace to one who has died so their sentence in purgatory is shortened (depending on how much one paid for the indulgence).

On a scale of 1-10, how often do you try and earn God's grace through good deeds and hard work?

1   2   3   4   5   6   7   8   9   10

SOLA FIDE—FAITH ALONE

> For by grace you have been saved through faith. And this is not your own doing; it is the gift of God, not a result of works, so that no one may boast. —*Ephesians 2:8-9*

We are justified—declared to be right with God—through faith alone. This sola is perhaps the cornerstone of the Reformation. Luther's struggle with his own sin, and his continued feeling of being an absolute wretch, reminded him that faith was all he had. He couldn't offer anything else. Knees on the ground, palms in the air—he had faith that God saved him, and that was his only hope.

Why is it important to understand that faith is a gift from God, not something we've done for ourselves?

SOLUS CHRISTUS—CHRIST ALONE

> Jesus said to him, "I am the way, and the truth, and the life. No one comes to the Father except through me." —*John 14:6*

There is no Christianity without Christ. There is no grace without Christ. There is no faith without Christ. Frankly, there is no Scripture without Christ, because Scripture is about Him (John 5:39). When it comes to salvation, it's Christ alone.

Why do you think "Christ alone" is an unpopular message today, even at times among Christians?

SOLI DEO GLORIA—GLORY TO GOD ALONE

> The heavens declare the glory of God, and the sky above proclaims his handiwork. —*Psalm 19:1*

We noted earlier that *sola fide* might be the cornerstone of the Reformation. If that's the case, *soli Deo gloria* might be the mortar that holds the stones together. God gets all the glory, not us. We're just blessed to be able to look up and see the heavens declaring His glory.

God's glory is a way of describing His perfect character and the reason He receives praise and credit for all things. In the margin, jot down three ways you try to share glory with God.

DIGGING DEEPER

Belief is an interesting thing. Everyone believes in something, right? Not just normal beliefs, like grass is green or the sky is blue. Everyone believes in deeper truths, like goodness and beauty and love and purpose.

As Christians, our beliefs go even further. We confess and believe certain things about God and about how the universe does (or doesn't) work. In other words, we don't believe in a generic, watered-down God.

As we've mentioned already in this session, our beliefs lead to our actions. According to Paul, what we confess with our mouths and believe in our hearts is a matter of salvation, of eternity (Rom. 10:9). The 95 theses were a blaring call for the church to reform some of its beliefs, because the church directly impacted people's lives not just immediately, but forever.

An example we discussed earlier this week is the selling of indulgences, in which people could buy certificates from the church in exchange for less punishment for their sins in the afterlife. Someone might say, "Jesus is the only one who can take away the punishment for sins, so who cares if people thought indulgences did something for them?" It seems kind of harmless, right?

These indulgences minimized the importance of trusting wholly in Christ for salvation, and we don't mix in false beliefs with right beliefs. Scripture is our authority, and we believe what it teaches. So we don't give God 99 percent worship and throw in a few indulgences just in case. It's slavery to believe that anything other than God can forgive sins and erase the punishment for them. The Church in Luther's day was selling grace, but grace is free—you can't buy it.

Remember, God isn't calling us to an ignorant faith. Scripture is a never-ending treasure chest of God-centered, life-changing truth. Our faith should not be blind—it should be seeking more and more understanding about the glorious God we serve. We should center our lives on the key truths He has laid out for us. And that's where the five solas come in.

Read James 1:22-25. How does this passage provide a balance for all we've discussed this week?

SCRIPTURE ALONE

HOW DO YOU KNOW?

Take a few minutes to jot down a few facts you know to be true.

Once your group has some potential answers, ask yourselves how you actually know any of those things to be true. Whatever reasons or rationale you give in support, how do you know that is true? Could you be wrong? Could you be mistaken? When pushed to support their beliefs and what they believe to be true, people often end up falling back on the simple phrase, "I just know it!"

For a lot of people, not having a solid foundation for their beliefs causes them to ultimately fall back to what they know in their hearts, what they see or feel with their senses, or what some authority figure has told them. We all have some ultimate authority we trust to give us truth—our senses, logic and reason, our families, or tradition. Whatever it is, we all have something we trust *just because.* For Christians, that final, ultimate authority is the Bible, God's Word to us.

THE BIG IDEA

What is asserted without the Scriptures or proven revelation may be held as an opinion, but need not be believed. —Martin Luther[1]

Reading the Bible was the primary spark in Luther's transformation from Catholic monk to revolutionary. As we saw last week, he stood before the leaders of the church and proclaimed,

> I am bound by the Scriptures I have quoted and my conscience is captive to the Word of God. I cannot and will not recant anything, since it is neither safe nor right to go against conscience to the Word of God. I cannot and will not recant anything, since it is neither safe nor right to go against conscience.[2]

When Luther began to see that the Church's practice was not lining up with God's Word, he had a choice to make: suppress his conscience or listen to it. As an aspiring priest and preacher, he felt the weight of being faithful to God's Word. He once wrote, "It is a glory which every preacher may claim, to be able to say with full confidence of heart: 'This trust have I toward God in Christ, that what I teach and preach is truly the Word of God.'"[3]

How have you responded to the misuse of power, either in your own life or someone else's?

Why should we submit to God's authority above all others?

THE AUTHORITY OF SCRIPTURE

All Scripture is breathed out by God and profitable for teaching, for reproof, for correction, and for training in righteousness, that the man of God may be complete, equipped for every good work. —2 Timothy 3:16-17

What are five sources of authority in your life today? Rank them in order, with the number one spot given to your most influential authority and down from there.

Saying that Scripture is the ultimate authority isn't well received in today's Western world. For many, science is often seen as the supreme authority, capable of giving us all the answers we seek about the world and our place in it. However, any intellectually honest scientist will say such fascinations simply aren't true.

Many others just turn to themselves when it comes to having a final and ultimate authority. They think of themselves as being clever enough to trust in their own reasoning skills to determine what truth is. In fact, there were entire generations that thought this way during the time period of the Enlightenment, but this type of thinking was eventually proven wrong and naive in the 20th century.

What does 2 Timothy 3:16-17 say about the origin and authority of Scripture?

If your words, thoughts, and actions reflect what you believe about Scripture's authority in your life, how much authority does Scripture have over you?

No Authority   Total Authority

| 1 | 2 | 3 | 4 | 5 | 6 | 7 | 8 | 9 | 10 |

In what ways can you give the Bible more authority in your life?

If God is the ultimate authority, the good and true King, then His words are good and true. He is perfect, so His Word is perfect. His commands are right and our obedience to them is right. No pope, president, king, or best-selling self-help book has more authority than God's Word. That also means that no matter what a leader does, God's Word has the final say.

For the word of God is living and active, sharper than any two-edged sword, piercing to the division of soul and of spirit, of joints and of marrow, and discerning the thoughts and intentions of the heart. And no creature is hidden from his sight, but all are naked and exposed to the eyes of him to whom we must give account. —*Hebrews 4:12-13*

Look at Hebrews 4:12-13 again. Highlight the words that describe God's Word.

Why is it important to recognize these things about Scripture?

BECOMING KINGS

To Luther, the Pope was more like a bad king than a good pastor. He abused his power and sought to control the people. The Word of God no longer controlled the Church—its leader did. A church that minimizes the Word is not a church at all; it's a train without tracks, a winding mountain road without guardrails.

The danger for us is to try and become kings ourselves, rather than turning to God and His Word for wisdom. Some of us want to be the kings of our schools, the kings of our neighborhoods, and the kings over our siblings. Some of us want to be the kings of our fantasy football leagues, or the kings on the field.

Kings stand above everyone else, receiving praise and reverence from everyone around them. Nothing is withheld from kings, after all. They never come in second place, and they never have to give in to another's needs. Kings have the power to fix stuff, including their own lives. It's good to be king.

In what ways do you try to control your own life?

Jot down three ways trying to take control of your life has backfired.

Now list three ways giving control to God has blessed you.

We're always either wanting to be king or looking to imperfect people to lead us perfectly. Our kings never fulfill us. We look outwardly in our culture or inwardly to ourselves, but we rarely look to the King we already have. And we rarely turn to His Word to collect the truth He has left there: God is King and you are not—and that's a good thing.

WHY DON'T WE READ THE BIBLE?

According to the Barna Group, there are several reasons people don't read the Bible—primarily because they don't have enough time or struggle to relate to the language. The statistics showed that 88 percent of American households own a Bible, but only 37 percent of people read it once a week or more.[4] No doubt, their frustration with trying to understand words, phrases, and concepts in Scripture is reasonable, but as most preachers have already told their congregations—people have plenty of time to read, but they simply don't want to make the effort.

In the end, our struggle with Bible reading is often not because of time or effort or ability, but because we don't expect to meet God there. We know at some level that God spoke in His Word, but we don't fully understand that God's still speaks to us through His Word. In short, we don't know what happens to us when we read it. We don't understand how God works on us through His Word.

GOSPEL APPLICATION

THE GREATEST STORY EVER TOLD

Let nobody suppose that he has tasted the Holy Scriptures sufficiently unless he has ruled over the churches with the prophets for a hundred years. —*Martin Luther*[5]

This quote reminds us that we will never fully exhaust the Word. It's a diamond we can see and appreciate, but never fully uncover. Its words tell a story like no other. *Star Wars* is great. Superhero movies are spellbinding. But they're all copies; they're lesser stories of a greater story. And God's Word will captivate us like those stories only when we realize that God meets with us on its pages. We will agree with John Calvin, that our thoughts and words should be conformed to Scripture, where God Himself speaks.[6] We need God to speak to us, but we don't always believe He does.

Reflecting on what you've read about Scripture so far, list three reasons "Scripture alone" is so crucial to Christian living.

THE WORD DOES IT ALL

I simply taught, preached, and wrote God's Word; otherwise I did nothing. ... [T]he Word so greatly weakened the papacy that never a prince or emperor did such damage to it. I did nothing. The Word did it all. —*Martin Luther*[7]

In this quote, we can see the way God's Word gripped Luther. As we've examined already, Scripture itself is what led Luther to question the Roman Catholic Church of the day. The Word absolutely floored him, and yet he didn't see the same reverence in his own Church tradition. The Pope exercised similar, if not the same, power over Christians as the Bible did.

What's interesting is that, in the end, Luther took no real credit for the Reformation. Instead, he said that "the Word did it all."

Why did Luther give credit to God's Word even though he did so much, participated in so many debates, and was even persecuted for his faith?

In what areas are we tempted to take credit for things God has provided?

Never	Rarely	Sometimes	All the time

TAKING THE WORD TO OTHERS

And they devoted themselves to the apostles' teaching and the fellowship, to the breaking of bread and the prayers. And awe came upon every soul, and many wonders and signs were being done through the apostles. And all who believed were together and had all things in common. And they were selling their possessions and belongings and distributing the proceeds to all, as any had need. And day by day, attending the temple together and breaking bread in their homes, they received their food with glad and generous hearts, praising God and having favor with all the people. And the Lord added to their number day by day those who were being saved. —*Acts 2:42-47*

The apostles were commissioned by Jesus to share His Word with the world (Matt. 28:18-20). Though Acts tells us that they suffered extreme persecution for doing so, why did they continue to preach His Word anyway?

Jot down at least one way sharing God's Word might cause a struggle or interference in your day-to-day life.

God's Word empowered the lives of these believers. Being sacrificially generous is difficult. Sharing our possessions and letting people into our homes can be exhausting. These early Christians no doubt struggled with the same sins of pride and selfishness as we do now, but they let God's Word have the final say. The apostles' teaching pushed them to live sacrificial lives for the sake of the gospel.

The gospel is the greatest unity we can offer, because it saves anyone and everyone who believes it, bringing believers into the same body of Christ. It offends, yes—but it also unites. Like Luther and like the early Christians in Acts, we should be emboldened by the power of God's Word to take the gospel to our living rooms, our neighborhoods, and to the ends of the Earth. We shouldn't have dinner with Sally next door and show her how righteous we are, trying to make her more like us. No, we should show her the character of Christ and the truth of God's Word.

How often do you find yourself apologizing for or minimizing what the Bible says?

What keeps you from believing that God's Word does the work, not you?

List three ways you can begin to point to God's Word rather than yourself in your life and in your relationships with others.

WHAT HAPPENS TO US WHEN WE READ THE BIBLE?

Let's revisit some foundational passages we've already discussed. Paul told Timothy:

> All Scripture is breathed out by God and profitable for teaching, for reproof, for correction, and for training in righteousness, that the man of God may be complete, equipped for every good work. —*2 Timothy 3:16-17*

Notice the verbs: Scripture is inspired by God and is profitable. They are active verbs, not verbs describing some distant time when God's Word meant something to some ancient people. Pair this with the powerful phrase in Hebrews 4:12-13:

> For the word of God is living and active, sharper than any two-edged sword, piercing to the division of soul and of spirit, of joints and of marrow, and discerning the thoughts and intentions of the heart. And no creature is hidden from his sight, but all are naked and exposed to the eyes of him to whom we must give account. —*Hebrews 4:12-13*

Again, notice: the Word of God is living and is effective and is able to judge the ideas and thoughts of the heart. If Jesus is the Word of God (John 1:1) and He's not dead, then the power of God's Word on the pages of Scripture isn't dead either. If the Holy Spirit speaks through the Word (2 Pet. 1:21), the Bible still has a heartbeat. The Word is alive! Luther interpreted Scripture as something that was applicable to him that day, at that time. The Church wasn't obeying God's Word, and the Bible told Luther so.

Before reading this section, how would you have described the Bible?

What gives Scripture its power today, in the here and now? How does that affect the way you approach it?

Captive to God's Word, the Holy Spirit led Luther to understand important truths about theology and the Christian life. Through the illumination of the Holy Spirit, our spiritual eyes are opened to the supernatural, life-giving truth of God's living Word, too. When we open its pages, the Bible speaks to us and calls on us to "taste and see that the Lᴏʀᴅ is good" (Ps. 34:8). The Bible, in a very real sense, lets us into the mind of God:

But, as it is written, "What no eye has seen, nor ear heard, nor the heart of man imagined, what God has prepared for those who love him"—these things God has revealed to us through the Spirit. For the Spirit searches everything, even the depths of God. For who knows a person's thoughts except the spirit of that person, which is in him? So also no one comprehends the thoughts of God except the Spirit of God. Now we have received not the spirit of the world, but the Spirit who is from God, that we might understand the things freely given us by God. And we impart this in words not taught by human wisdom but taught by the Spirit, interpreting spiritual truths to those who are spiritual. *—1 Corinthians 2:9-13*

Want to know what God thinks? Not just what He *thought*, but what He *thinks*? Open the Bible. Luther understood the Bible's power to change lives, because his own life was changed by it. His reading of Romans 1:17 changed the course of his life, and he was never the same. And because of that, neither was the Church. Neither are we.

GRACE ALONE

START

Before you dig into this session, read the following story.

A local doughnut shop used to give a free doughnut to students who brought in their report cards, marked with *A's*. One day, a brother and sister brought their report cards home, only to discover the brother had one *B* on his report card, and he wouldn't get a free doughnut. The sister felt bad about the fact that her brother wouldn't get a doughnut. She walked to the counter, picked out her treat, walked over to the table where her brother waited, and handed him the doughnut. No "you owe me," no holding her gift over his head, or gloating about the prize she'd earned. She received the gift of a doughnut, and turned around to give that gift to her brother. Though he did none of the work, he still received the reward—he received a gift he didn't earn.

Would you have done the same in this situation? Why or why not?

Though this story is far more simple than God's gift of grace, it demonstrates a similar principle. Jesus lived a perfect life. His card would have been filled with *A's* and pluses. He faced temptation without giving in, He was perfectly patient, perfectly kind, and perfectly obedient all the way to the cross. He did the work for us.

And there, on the cross, He paid the final price of all that we owed for our sin. This was a hefty price to pay—pain, suffering, death, and most of all, a moment of separation from His Father. He went through all of that for us. Yet, when He turns to us and offers His gift of grace, He doesn't close His fingers across it and tell us to work harder to earn it. He holds His hands open, freely offering a gift we could never earn or repay.

How does it affect you to know that you could never earn salvation or repay Jesus for what He did for you on the cross?

THE BIG IDEA

We are beggars: this is true. —*Martin Luther*[1]

You might be surprised to know that Luther taught salvation by grace alone while he was a Catholic monk—and it wasn't all that controversial.[2] However, "grace alone" didn't mean what Luther would eventually consider "by grace alone." The Church taught that grace did not save completely, but rather *prepared* people to be saved. Luther the monk said that grace alone is the gasoline to propel the car of salvation; Luther the reformer said that grace alone is the entire car.

Luther's view of "grace alone" became biblical as he moved away from the man-made traditions of the Catholic Church of his day. He later commented on the shift in his teaching:

> It's true. I was a good monk and kept my order so strictly that I could say that if ever a monk could get to heaven through monastic discipline, I should have entered in. All my companions in the monastery who knew me would bear me out in this. For if it had gone on much longer, I would have martyred myself to death, what with vigils, prayers, readings, and other works. . . . And yet my conscience would not give me certainty, but I always doubted and said, "You didn't do that right. You weren't contrite enough. You left that out of your confession." The more I tried to remedy an uncertain, weak and troubled conscience with human traditions, the more daily I found it more uncertain, weaker and more troubled.[3]

Much like Paul in Philippians 3, Luther followed all the rules and kept all the doctrines of the Church. But rules don't save us—grace does. True grace is found in Christ, not in personal morality and strength. Here is a piece of Paul's story:

> I myself have reason for confidence in the flesh also. If anyone else thinks he has reason for confidence in the flesh, I have more: circumcised on the eighth day, of the people of Israel, of the tribe of Benjamin, a Hebrew of Hebrews; as to the law, a Pharisee; as to zeal, a persecutor of the church; as to righteousness under the law, blameless. But whatever gain I had, I counted as loss for the sake of Christ. —*Philippians 3:4-7*

In what ways do you treat grace like an add-on rather than sufficient?

As a Christian, how does your story relate to Paul's?

Before this session, how did you view grace and works?

Why was it so important for Luther to distinguish between works and grace?

Luther and the Reformers realized that teaching people to work harder or pay higher prices for grace is not the gospel. After all, the gospel means good news. And we all know from experience—we're toast without the grace of God. We sin every day. Telling us to be perfect would be bad news. Really, really bad news.

The truth is, we're all on the same playing field. "All have sinned and fall short of the glory of God" (Rom. 3:23). The nicest person you've ever met and the most hateful person you've ever met have one big thing in common—without God's grace, they're hopeless.

THE GOOD NEWS OF GRACE

For all have sinned and fall short of the glory of God, and are justified by his grace as a gift, through the redemption that is in Christ Jesus.
—*Romans 3:23-24*

Jot down three ways you have experienced God's unmerited grace in your life.

When you received this grace, were you quick to thank God for it? Why or why not?

There are many who believe that salvation is by grace through faith in Jesus, but live as if it is all up to them. In other words, they believe that God has saved them, but they don't live like it. As Paul said in Galatians 3:3, we are foolish if we think God's work in our lives (which began by the work of the Holy Spirit) could be completed by our own strength. But that's the thing: the Holy Spirit begins the work and completes it, all by grace. As Paul said:

In him you also, when you heard the word of truth, the gospel of your salvation, and believed in him, were sealed with the promised Holy Spirit, who is the guarantee of our inheritance until we acquire possession of it, to the praise of his glory.
—*Ephesians 1:13-14*

THE GREAT CONFLICT IN OUR HEARTS

How does grace influence the way you handle conflict with others?

Circle where you are on the line below when it comes to accepting blame in a conflict.

Never   Rarely   Sometimes   All the time
|_____|_____|_____|

"None is righteous, no, not one; no one understands; no one seeks for God. All have turned aside; together they have become worthless; no one does good, not even one." —*Romans 3:10-12*

On the average week, how often do you intentionally repent of your sins?

A. Less than once

B. Once

C. More than once

List three reasons you don't repent of a sin you regularly commit.

But the gospel gives us something better. The gospel tells us that God knows and loves every part of us, so there's no reason to hide. The gospel tells us we're transformed by the work that Jesus has already done when He died on the cross and rose again, so there's no reason to live in self-condemnation. The gospel tells us that we can love God and others, not ourselves, because Jesus sacrificed His own life for us. The gospel tells us that "being true to ourselves" means understanding that we are sinners in need of grace. The gospel is good news for bad people.

A LIFE OF REPENTANCE

On the cross, Jesus said, "It is finished" (John 19:30). And He really meant it. Everything that needed to be done, Jesus did. He gave us the gospel to make us new and to continue making us new. He gave us His righteousness and took on punishment for our sins (Rom. 8:1-4). God knows that sin is strong—so strong that it's impossible to defeat it on our own. More than that, sometimes we like to sin; it feels good or gets us what we want in the moment. That's why Jesus finished the work. We don't have to measure up to anything because He already measured up. We don't have to do anything because Jesus already did everything.

What other ways do you try to get to God other than through Jesus (who is the only way)?

How often do you try and do the work of pleasing God that Jesus has already done on the cross?

The gospel doesn't simply make you a better person or a person who suddenly has the power to work a little harder at being good. Your life in Christ is not simply better—it's totally new! Your life is not about being better, acting better, or believing better advice; it's about understanding how much better Jesus is than anything else in the universe. It's about grace alone changing your life.

Circle where you are on the line below when it comes to how often you try and earn grace.

Never	Rarely	Sometimes	All the time

How does God's gift of grace challenge your attempts at earning grace?

Paul's transformation from a killer of Christians to an apostle of Christ was radical but didn't happen overnight. He almost certainly never killed another Christian after he met Christ, but life wasn't suddenly perfect. Paul told the Corinthians that he still needed to be reminded of grace:

To keep me from becoming conceited because of the surpassing greatness of the revelations, a thorn was given me in the flesh, a messenger of Satan to harass me, to keep me from becoming conceited. Three times I pleaded with the Lord about this, that it should leave me. But he said to me, "My grace is sufficient for you, for my power is made perfect in weakness." Therefore I will boast all the more gladly of my weaknesses, so that the power of Christ may rest upon me. For the sake of Christ, then, I am content with weaknesses, insults, hardships, persecutions, and calamities. For when I am weak, then I am strong. —2 Corinthians 12:7-10

We are strongest not when we're standing up to giants, but when we're kneeling down before God. True strength is found in a life of repentance. Grace knocks us off our feet so we can sit at the foot of the cross.

GOSPEL APPLICATION

The whole teaching of the Gospel is a sure demonstration that what God has promised will certainly be performed. For the Gospel is now an accomplished fact: the One who was promised to the patriarchs, and to the whole race, has now been given to us, and in him we have the assurance of all our hope. —Huldrych Zwingli[4]

We've discussed this before but it bears repeating: The Reformation wasn't merely about Luther's frustration. It was about everyday people like you and me, who were being taught that they didn't have direct access to God or that God's grace wasn't sufficient for them. Luther couldn't stand by and watch the Church shackle people with works-based salvation.

Today, when we ask people how they can "get to heaven," they often respond with some answer like, "Be a good person," "Love others," or "Treat people how you want to be treated." Those answers sound pretty good, don't they? The world would be a much better place if everyone lived that way. But even if everyone lived that way, it wouldn't promise them eternity with God.

So, when we step through our front doors and into the world, what are we telling others about God's grace? Are we living lives that are shaped by the gospel and empowered by the Spirit and reflect God's grace, mercy, and love? If the world believes they can build their own way to heaven simply by having good intentions, how are we who have been saved by grace alone giving them better news?

Reflecting on what you've read about God's grace so far, list three reasons "grace alone" is so crucial to Christian living.

THE GIFT OF GRACE

While they long for you and pray for you, because of the surpassing grace of God upon you. Thanks be to God for his inexpressible gift! —2 Corinthians 9:14-15

When we think about the Reformers' work toward restoring the good news of the gospel to the church, we see a high level of unselfishness. Were they perfect? No, of course not! But they were on a mission that was bigger than themselves. When you understand grace, you realize that God's mission to save sinners is bigger than you.

God is the giver of all good gifts (Jas. 1:17). Grace is indescribable (2 Cor. 9:14-15). We can try to describe it. We can talk about how grace is free, how it's undeserved, or how it can't be bought—but we can't fully describe it. It's hard to put into words something that we can't fully grasp.

Still, we shouldn't be afraid to tell others about grace. We have to understand that God's grace isn't something we can bottle up and pour over someone else's head—it must come from God. He gives us grace to share the gospel of grace and commands us to point others toward it (Matt. 28:19).

Who in your life needs to know about God's grace?

In what ways can you demonstrate grace and tell that person about God's grace in your own life?

Of all the qualities that point to the gift of grace, it might be most appropriate to point out that grace is unselfish. Think about it: God the Father sent His one and only Son into the world to save us (John 3:16). Grace wasn't just an idea for God—grace had a Name. As John 1:14 tells us, Jesus is "full of grace and truth."

Why does sacrificially showing grace make us uncomfortable?

In what ways can you sacrificially show grace to others the way God has shown sacrificial grace to you?

WHERE GRACE IS FOUND

Let us then with confidence draw near to the throne of grace, that we may receive mercy and find grace to help in time of need. —Hebrews 4:16

The world thinks it can find grace in something other than God. Even the Catholic Church in Luther's time taught this. They said the Church had some grace too, if you had the money or the ability. "Come to church to receive God's grace" doesn't sound so bad, does it? That idea seems harmless or even helpful until the church actually starts thinking grace comes from inside its doors rather than from God Himself.

As Christians, it's easy for us to accidentally feed others the lie that grace is found in us, in the church, or in good morals. But, trading out the idol of an immoral habit, such as drug use, for the habit of good church attendance isn't helpful. Acting like another person who is kind and does good things, or who might even be a Christian doesn't give us a better standing with God either. Grace doesn't say, "Trade out a good work for a better work," "Clean yourself up," or "Act more 'Christian.'" Instead, grace says, "You bring nothing to the table, but Christ has brought everything to the table for you."

According to Hebrews 4:16, why should we approach the throne of grace "with confidence"?

How does our access to the throne of grace impact our telling others about it?

Christ's work trumps your work. His work gives you rest—eternal, joyful, final rest (Heb. 4:1-11). So showing others God's grace isn't work. It's not knowing the right formula or memorizing the entire Bible. That would mean you've got the right tools to save someone, and you don't. Instead, you have God the Holy Spirit inside of you, working through you. Point others to Him—the only place that grace is found.

[God] desires all people to be saved and to come to the knowledge of the truth. —1 Timothy 2:3-4

Paul's statement to Timothy here is a simple one, and if there's one verse to keep in your mind at all times, it's this one. Why? Because it reminds us that no one is too far from God's salvation. God offers the gift of His grace to all people.

Commenting on this passage, John Calvin said, "There is no people and no rank in the world that is excluded from salvation; because God wishes that the gospel should be proclaimed to all without exception."[5]

This was a large part of Luther's problem with the Church. Grace was for everyone, everywhere, but the church was holding out on them. The Church kept grace in-house. They didn't tell people to merely "live a life of repentance," but to jump through complicated hoops to make sure they were saved. They shackled people with a gospel-less, works-based system.

Now, look at your own life. Do you create a system of works for those who are far from God or struggling in their faith? Do you tell them to clean up, straighten up, and get over it? Or indirectly, do you model for them a life of moral hard work? When they look at your life, they should be more amazed at the grace that's transforming you than the discipline you've mustered in being a "good person."

FAITH ALONE

START

Welcome to Session 4 of our study. Last week, we talked about the idea that God's grace alone saves us. Answer these questions in reflection.

In what ways did being more aware of God's grace impact your life this week?

In what ways did you show God's grace to others this week?

Choose a partner to work through the following activity before you dig into today's study:

One student will have the blindfold on, while the other will not be blindfolded. The blindfolded student will also be unable to talk, especially since the partner who is not blindfolded will be giving instructions to the blindfolded student.

The "seeing" student will not be allowed in the obstacle course or be able to physically guide his or her partner. The blindfolded student must avoid the cones (or whatever obstacles you have set) simply by trusting their partner's instructions. You can enact penalties for each time the blindfolded student touches a cone. The point is to demonstrate trusting someone else to guide you, even when you can't see.

The truth is, no relationship can thrive without trust. Your relationship with God is similar—without faith and trust in Him, the relationship simply doesn't exist. The only way to be made right with God is by grace alone, *through faith* alone, in Christ alone.

This week, find out what "faith alone" truly means.

THE BIG IDEA

No one can come to me unless the Father who sent me draws him. And I will raise him up on the last day. —*John 6:44*

Justification by faith alone is perhaps the cornerstone of the Reformation. This sola is the exact point where the theological rubber meets the Reformation road. All the key truths for Luther and his followers rested on the idea that we can't contribute to our salvation. According to Luther, we can never forget this truth of the gospel:

> Here I must take counsel of the gospel. I must hearken to the gospel, which teacheth me, not what I ought to do...but what Jesus Christ the Son of God hath done for me ...that he suffered and died to deliver me from sin and death. The gospel willeth me to receive this, and to believe it. And this is the truth of the gospel. It is also the principal article of all Christian doctrine, wherein the knowledge of all godliness consisteth. Most necessary it is, therefore, that we should know this article well, teach it unto others, and beat it into their heads continually.[1]

The Church had forgotten the gospel. They had forgotten the *alone* side of the equation. They were adding so many ingredients to the recipe that it no longer looked like the gospel. Luther's remedy for their—and *our*—gospel amnesia was a simple one: Share it continually!

Jot down three ways you've recently tried to justify yourself.

Now, record three ways the gospel trumps those justifications.

THE HUMILITY OF FAITH

You'll notice that this session already sounds similar to the last session on grace alone. Luther taught that we are justified *by* grace alone *through* faith alone. In other words, it's only the grace of God that allows us sinners and rebels to have faith. Faith and grace are always tied together. We are saved by grace when we put our faith in Jesus Christ, but it's the work of grace that makes that faith genuine and alive.

Notice the connection between the two ideas here:

> By grace you have been saved through faith. And this is not your own doing; it is the gift of God, not a result of works, so that no one may boast. —*Ephesians 2:8-9*

What does it mean for faith to be a gift from God rather than something you've earned?

In what ways are you tempted to act prideful instead of humble about the forgiveness Christ has given you?

> Once you were not a people, but now you are God's people; once you had not received mercy, but now you have received mercy. —*1 Peter 2:10*

Read 1 Peter 2:10. What does this verse teach us about our relationship with God before mercy and after mercy?

CHRIST'S RIGHTEOUSNESS

A core belief in the Reformation's teaching on justification is the idea of Christ imputing, or crediting, His righteousness to us. His righteousness becomes our righteousness, so that our sinfulness is no longer how God judges us. In other words, when God looks at you, He sees Jesus' righteousness instead of your sin.

And this is why it's so dangerous to trust ourselves or anyone else for justification.

> Nor was it to offer himself repeatedly, as the high priest enters the holy places every year with blood not his own, for then he would have had to suffer repeatedly since the foundation of the world. But as it is, he has appeared once for all at the end of the ages to put away sin by the sacrifice of himself. —*Hebrews 9:25-27*

Why are we unable to be righteous on our own?

Circle where you are on the line below when it comes to how often you try to be righteous on your own.

Never   Rarely   Sometimes   All the time
|_____|_____|_____|

FAITH AND WORKS

If our own works can't justify us, we're left asking a pretty simple question: Why does anything we do matter? Isn't it true that our sins are washed away by grace through faith? Hasn't the whole point of this study been that works mean nothing to God? Well, not quite.

To be fair, these questions confused Luther too. He knew for sure that justification by faith alone was biblical and true, but he was perplexed by passages like this in the Book of James:

> What good is it, my brothers, if someone says he has faith but does not have works? Can that faith save him? If a brother or sister is poorly clothed and lacking in daily food, and one of you says to them, "Go in peace, be warmed and filled," without giving them the things needed for the body, what good is that? So also faith by itself, if it does not have works, is dead. But someone will say, "You have faith and I have works." Show me your faith apart from your works, and I will show you my faith by my works. You believe that God is one; you do well. Even the demons believe—and shudder! Do you want to be shown, you foolish person, that faith apart from works is useless? ... For as the body apart from the spirit is dead, so also faith apart from works is dead. —*James 2:14-20,26*

James said that "even the demons believe." How is true belief different from theirs?

Why is it necessary that works flow from faith?

Luther and James both agree: Faith without works is dead. There's no such thing as faith that people can't see. The gospel is so powerful that it changes us and so wonderful that we can't contain it.

THAT GRACE MAY ABOUND

Paul asked (and then answered) an interesting question in his letter to the Romans:

> Are we to continue in sin that grace may abound? By no means! How can we who died to sin still live in it? —*Romans 6:1-2*

Luther is right: Faith without works is a sign of malfunction. Faith is a gift from God, and God doesn't give us dead, powerless gifts. Faith actually *does* something. It's alive and powerful and transformative. By the power of the Holy Spirit, we are being conformed to the image of Christ (Rom. 8:29; 2 Cor. 3:18). If we have faith but our lives aren't on a path toward Christ-likeness, then something is wrong.

> How often do you give into a temptation because you know you'll be forgiven?

> On the other hand, how often do you rely on your own works apart from faith in Christ?

The takeaway from Luther is this: Works don't justify us, but works show that we're justified.

In the end, the goal of humanity is not only to be forgiven so we can get to heaven someday; it is primarily to be like Christ. God justifies us through Christ's work, not ours—which means *He* is the standard. Be like Him, and you are who you were made to be. And you can be like Him by faith alone.

JUSTIFIED TOWARD HOPE

> Since we have been justified by faith, we have peace with God through our Lord Jesus Christ. Through him we have also obtained access by faith into this grace in which we stand, and we rejoice in hope of the glory of God. Not only that, but we rejoice in our sufferings, knowing that suffering produces endurance, and endurance produces character, and character produces hope, and hope does not put us to shame, because God's love has been poured into our hearts through the Holy Spirit who has been given to us. —*Romans 5:1-5*

According to Paul, not only do we have peace with God through faith in Christ, but we now have a reason to rejoice and hope. This goes back to the fact that faith in Christ is not simply about forgiveness of sins, but about what faith does in our lives. Faith brings forgiveness; forgiveness brings peace; peace brings hope; hope brings endurance in suffering.

John Calvin argued that we must be continually reminded of our justification:

> [W]e would certainly find ourselves in a miserable condition if we had to again be afraid all of the time that God's grace could all of a sudden not be there for us anymore![2]

Calvin was right: How can we hope in God's promises if we're always terrified that He won't keep them? If God says He will save us, then we must trust Him because His promises come true. No relationship can thrive if there isn't trust.

How often do you have a hard time believing God's promises?

Why can we trust all of God's promises?

FAITH WORKS

Faith isn't about works, but faith works. Put simply: Faith causes our hearts to do good works. But these faith-driven, grace-empowered works aren't simply good deeds, like being kind, patient, or generous. Of course those things come along with it, but there's more. When asked what the greatest commandment is, Jesus replied that it's two-fold:

> You shall love the Lord your God with all your heart and with all your soul and with all your mind. This is the great and first commandment. And a second is like it: You shall love your neighbor as yourself. On these two commandments depend all the Law and the Prophets. —*Matthew 22:37-40*

What is the difference between a good deed and loving someone like Christ loves them?

Why is it important to understand this difference?

This is faith in action: to love God and love others. These two cannot be separated because our love for others actually flows from our faith in God. We can't look at others with love if we aren't looking up at God with love, knowing the love He sent down to us in Jesus.

GOSPEL APPLICATION

WHOSE JUSTIFICATION IS IT?

"The word is near you, in your mouth and in your heart" (that is, the word of faith that we proclaim); because, if you confess with your mouth that Jesus is Lord and believe in your heart that God raised him from the dead, you will be saved. For with the heart one believes and is justified, and with the mouth one confesses and is saved. For the Scripture says, "Everyone who believes in him will not be put to shame." For there is no distinction between Jew and Greek; for the same Lord is Lord of all, bestowing his riches on all who call on him. For "everyone who calls on the name of the Lord will be saved." —*Romans 10:8-13*

As we've discussed this week, it's not difficult to try to find justification for our own sins. We are self-serving to a fault. But when it comes to loving and serving others, it gets a little messier. It's easier to hide inside our houses to read and pray, but it's quite another to walk across the street and talk with a borderline stranger. It's not easy to give money to a ministry or give away something we cherish to someone who has nothing. But part of loving God is loving the people He created. Remember, the greatest commandment is to love God and love others.

There are plenty of ways to love others, but love doesn't stop with a smile or a donation. Love must ultimately lead others to a greater love than yours—the love of Christ. Romans 10:8-13 tells us clearly: *anyone* ("there is no distinction") who believes in Christ can be saved. Believe and confess. No additives.

Sometimes we make faith complicated, as though it needs to be faith plus extra beliefs or works. Why does Paul make it so simple (Rom. 10:8b-13)?

How does the simplicity of faith encourage us to share the gospel with others?

The Roman Catholic Church told people to follow a multi-step process to receive forgiveness of sins. If a person completed the task, God would forgive that person.[3] But the Reformers understood that justification for even the "smallest" sin doesn't come from our own effort.

Carrying the Reformers' convictions into our own lives, we shouldn't be telling people that they need more than simple faith to be justified before God. Of course, we are also not saying that simple faith is an easy believism, similar to the mental assent of demons. No, it is a deep seated faith that carries over from an internal trust and dependence upon God to a life of repentance and good works. The repentance and good works come from the saving faith; they don't create it.

For the Christian, inaction is not an option. We are drawn into God's love and then sent out to show it to the world. No one on this planet is as equipped as you are to show God's love, because God Himself lives inside of you through the Holy Spirit. No one can compete with that. Jesus told His disciples that not even the gates of hell stand a chance against God's gospel-carrying people (Matt. 16:18). When Jesus prayed to His Father, "Your kingdom come, your will be done, on earth as it is in heaven" (Matt. 6:10), He was asking for God's perfect will to be done here, on this sinful, broken planet. We've been given the good news in a bad news world and that should inspire us to join in with God in His plan to redeem sinners.

When we love others, we show them God's love. When we forgive others, we show them God's forgiveness. When we are patient with others, we show God's patience to others. When we tell others the truth, we show God's truth. When we sacrifice for others, we show Christ's sacrifice on the cross. Do you see that? There's always a connection. Our works are always a product of our faith in a perfect, just, and loving God. A life lived in light of justification by faith alone shows others the beauty that they too can be justified by faith alone.

> List three people who need to hear about God's offer to justify them by grace alone through faith alone in Christ.

DIGGING DEEPER

THE WEIGHT OF SIN AND THE PEACE OF CHRIST

If anyone would feel the greatness of sin he would not be able to go on living another moment; so great is the power of sin. —Martin Luther[4]

Luther wasn't saying sin is great, as in really good. Rather, he meant that sin is huge—it weighs on us like a million-ton stone made of guilt, shame, and frustration. Sometimes sin starts small with a simple desire that feels harmless. But sin doesn't play games.

Desire when it has conceived gives birth to sin, and sin when it is fully grown brings forth death. —James 1:15

According to James, sin is like a little baby that seems sweet and innocent at first, but grows up to be a deadly monster. Sin brings death (Rom. 6:23). This is what Luther meant when he said that we could not live another moment if we understood sin. Sin kills us—literally—and understanding it only makes that reality clearer.

Before reading the past few paragraphs, how would you have described sin?

After just this brief introduction, would you change your earlier definition?

CHRIST ALONE

START

Welcome to Session 5 of this study. Last week, we talked about the idea that faith alone justifies us. Answer these questions in reflection.

In what ways did our session on faith alone change the way you view your relationship with God?

How did learning more about faith alone impact your relationships with others?

When children learn colors, they learn how to tell blue from orange. When they learn shapes, they learn that they (literally) can't fit a square peg in a round hole. Over time, all of us learn to live in the tension that some things simply are what they are. Day is not the same as night; being happy is not the same as being furious; and frozen yogurt is definitely not ice cream.

Christianity is no different. Christians can't agree with culture's idea that many paths lead to God. Salvation through anyone but Christ might as well be frozen yogurt calling itself ice cream. Luther preached this truth boldly as he saw the Catholic Church seating the Pope and other leaders too close to Christ's throne: "Any true Christian, living or dead, possesses a God-given share in all the benefits of Christ and the church, even without indulgence letters."[1] Simply put: Through Christ alone, Christians have all they need for salvation and every blessing that comes with it.

THE BIG IDEA

The summary of the gospel is that our Lord Christ, true Son of God, has made known to us the will of his Heavenly Father and has redeemed us from death and reconciled us to God by his guiltlessness. Therefore, Christ is the only way to salvation of all who were, are now, or shall be.
—*Huldrych Zwingli*[2]

When asked about how a person can inherit eternal life, Jesus usually gave a pretty stock answer.

I am the way, and the truth, and the life. No one comes to the Father except through me. If you had known me, you would have known my Father also. From now on you do know him and have seen him. —*John 14:6-7*

He made a clear statement here: The only way a person can come to the Father (be saved and have eternal life) is through Jesus. He didn't say, "I am one of many ways, one of many truths, and one of many lives." He also didn't say, "No one can come to the Father except through me, unless you're a really good person." There is one truth, one way, and one life that leads to salvation—Jesus Christ.

Notice these statements earlier in the Gospel of John:

In the beginning was the Word, and the Word was with God, and the Word was God. He was in the beginning with God. All things were made through him, and without him was not any thing made that was made. In him was life, and the life was the light of men. ... No one has ever seen God; the only God, who is at the Father's side, he has made him known. —*John 1:1-4,18*

What do these verses communicate about Jesus' identity?

God so loved the world, that he gave his only Son, that whoever believes in him should not perish but have eternal life. For God did not send his Son into the world to condemn the world, but in order that the world might be saved through him. —*John 3:16-17*

What do these verses communicate about God's means of salvation?

No one can come to me unless the Father who sent me draws him. And I will raise him up on the last day. It is written in the Prophets, "And they will all be taught by God." Everyone who has heard and learned from the Father comes to me—not that anyone has seen the Father except he who is from God; he has seen the Father. Truly, truly, I say to you, whoever believes has eternal life. —*John 6:44-47*

What do these verses communicate about Jesus' role in salvation?

Even though Jesus pointed back to the Father as the One who sent Him, Jesus is the only One the Father sent and the only One through whom we can go to the Father. Their relationship opens the door for our relationship with them. It is through Christ alone that we can be saved.

Go back to John 1:1-4,18; 3:16-17; and 6:44-47 and circle all occurrences of the words "Father" and "Son."

List three ways the relationship between the Father and Son impacts us.

GOD IN THE FLESH

When Jesus was born in a manger some two thousand years ago, He didn't just make an impact from that point forward, His birth uprooted history and turned it on its head. Things in the past came to mean something different. He was not just some special child. He wasn't merely the heir to a great kingdom. Rather, as Matthew 1:23 tells us, He was "Immanuel (which means, God with us)."

Luther and the Reformers couldn't escape the truth of Christ alone, because the Bible wouldn't let them. Looking for other gods for salvation instead of the God-man Jesus was full of problems. None of those false gods were sent by the Father; therefore, they couldn't lead back to the Father.

Why is it important that Jesus is God?

When you think of Jesus, do you more often think of Him as God in the flesh or as a nice, moral teacher? Explain.

THE RESURRECTED SAVIOR

> If Christ has not been raised, your faith is futile and you are still in your sins. Then those also who have fallen asleep in Christ have perished. If in Christ we have hope in this life only, we are of all people most to be pitied. But in fact Christ has been raised from the dead, the firstfruits of those who have fallen asleep. For as by a man came death, by a man has come also the resurrection of the dead. For as in Adam all die, so also in Christ shall all be made alive. —*1 Corinthians 15:17-22*

Imagine for a second that Jesus died on the cross and then stayed dead—He never walked out of the tomb. Let's say that to this day, His bone dust is still in a grave somewhere in the Middle East. Would that matter? He died as a substitute for our sins, so isn't that enough?

According to Paul in this passage, Jesus death is only half of the story. Yes, He died for our sins. (Praise God!) But more than that, He rose from the dead. Adam brought death into the world, so somebody had to bring life back to the world. Jesus staying dead wouldn't really solve the problem of death. He would be just another man in a six-foot hole.

But Jesus came back to life so we could have eternal life, rather than the eternal death we received from Adam. Mankind was never supposed to die. Genesis 3–Revelation 20 is a story of sin and death, but God wants us to live in a Genesis 1-2 and Revelation 21-22 world, where sin and death don't exist and people are right with God. In Christ alone, we can live eternally with our Creator just like we were made to.

Why is it important that Jesus not only died for our sins, but also rose from the dead?

Why can't a priest or pastor pray a special prayer to save us?

Why can't we save ourselves?

CHRIST IN ME

I have been crucified with Christ. It is no longer I who live, but Christ who lives in me. And the life I now live in the flesh I live by faith in the Son of God, who loved me and gave himself for me. —Galatians 2:20

First things first: Our source of joy is not our own efforts or circumstances, but the unwavering person of Christ. Our joy is bundled up in God's grace and mercy shown to us through Christ. We are united with Christ because He lives in us. But there's even more to our union with Christ. It's not simply that He lives in us, though He does, and it's not simply about how we see God through the work of Christ. Our union with Christ is also about how God sees us through the work of Christ.

Circle where you are on the line below when it comes to how often you feel like Christ lives within you.

Never   Rarely   Sometimes   All the time

In what ways does Galatians 2:20 change your outlook on Christ living within you?

UNION SPARKS COMMUNION

The Reformers saw something that the church apparently missed—our salvation is anchored in Christ alone. Though we are all "justified and at the same time sinners," Christ alone is the justifier and at the same time sinless. Because of that, our union with Christ should lead to communion with Christ.

How does the Holy Spirit's work impact our union with Christ?

The Holy Spirit is God. If that's true, how does it affect our reading of Ephesians 1:13-14?

We have everything we need in Christ alone. We are saved by grace through faith in Him. His life is now our life. His righteousness is now our righteousness. His gifts from the Father are now our gifts. The only offering we can lay before Jesus is the sin that nailed

Him to the cross. Because Jesus is righteous, holy, good, and wanted to unite us with Himself, He went to the cross with joy (Heb. 12:1-2).

This love that unites us should carry us into full communion with Him. In other words, His love is so mighty that it can and should overtake our desire to disobey and ignore Him. Next, we will take a look at a metaphor Scripture uses to describe our union and communion with Christ: marriage.

GOSPEL APPLICATION

Faith must be taught correctly, namely, that by it you are so cemented to Christ that He and you are as one person, which cannot be separated but remains attached to him forever... —*Martin Luther*[3]

You might get a hundred different answers if you asked random people on the street, "Who is Jesus?" You'd be hard-pressed in America to find someone who didn't at least know His name. However, it would be difficult to find people who could truly express how the Bible describes Him. Jesus might be the most misunderstood and doubted man of all-time, as some call Him merely a good teacher and others say He is a made-up character in a fiction book.

But if He really was who said He was, our only response is worship. The question before us is whether or not we will go and tell the world who He really is. In his writing, Luther nailed it: "faith must be taught correctly," and union with Christ is the cornerstone truth of our faith. The gospel rests on the idea that God is redeeming all things through Christ, and therefore, salvation cannot come to anyone without them first being united to Him. Only the Redeemer can redeem.

How does union and communion with Christ affect the way we view those around us?

Follow the pattern of the sound words that you have heard from me, in the faith and love that are in Christ Jesus. By the Holy Spirit who dwells within us, guard the good deposit entrusted to you. —*2 Timothy 1:13-14*

In Christ alone, we find our hope. We are called to bring the good news to a world filled with bad news, telling them that Jesus is more than a good teacher. If we are truly guarding the good deposit and teaching it correctly to others, then we are primarily telling them about the hope found in uniting with Christ by grace through faith.

Jot down three false gospels the world teaches today.

Now, explain how the true gospel exposes as false each of these so-called gospels.

WHY WE AVOID SHARING THE GOSPEL

There are several reasons we don't share the gospel. For some of us, it's a matter of being too busy to really think about it. For others, it's more about fear of looking silly or being disliked. Whatever the excuse, we ultimately don't share the gospel because we forget the beauty of being united with Christ. When we forget our union with Christ and all the benefits that relationship entails, we don't feel the urgency to share about that gift with others.

What struggles in your life cause you lose sight of eternity?

What does the doctrine of Christ alone say about our eternal perspective?

ALL AUTHORITY

Jesus came and said to them, "All authority in heaven and on earth has been given to me. Go therefore and make disciples of all nations, baptizing them in the name of the Father and of the Son and of the Holy Spirit, teaching them to observe all that I have commanded you. And behold, I am with you always, to the end of the age."
—Matthew 28:18-20

A lot of people are scared of sharing the gospel because they think they have to be an authority on the gospel. But in reality, believing that Christ alone saves people is more compelling than any seminary degree. If we put the authority to save people on ourselves, we're heading into a suicide mission in which everyone jumps on our shoulders and we get crushed under their weight. Only Jesus Christ has the authority, not us.

In what ways does the doctrine of Christ alone make evangelism less scary?

Matthew 28 is the last chapter of Matthew's Gospel, and this commission was the last thing Jesus said to His disciples before He went back to heaven. As with anyone, the last thing a person says to you is often the most important. So when Jesus sent out His disciples for the last time, He didn't just tell them to go—He told them to go in His authority.

In what ways can you reflect Christ to those around you?

Why is it important to not only reflect Christ, but also guard the good deposit?

Name three people in your life who need to hear the good news of Christ alone.

DIGGING DEEPER

If, because of one man's trespass, death reigned through that one man, much more will those who receive the abundance of grace and the free gift of righteousness reign in life through the one man Jesus Christ. —*Romans 5:17*

Last week, we discussed the idea of justification by faith alone, and we learned that Christ's righteousness is the only righteousness that God will accept. As God in the flesh, Jesus carries the perfection and holiness of God. As mankind in the flesh, we carry the imperfection and sin of Adam. However, Jesus didn't walk the earth as a hologram of God; He was a real, flesh-and-bones man.

Before sin entered the world, mankind was perfect. Adam and Eve lived in perfect harmony with God and with each other. But Adam brought sin and death into the world. Now we all, from the beginning, inherit a sinful nature from our first father. One sin brought death and destruction into the world. One sin was all it took to separate God from His people, because sin cannot dwell with God—not even one.

But in order to bring us back to God, there had to be a man who could be a mediator—a go-between—that could bridge the gap between God and His people. Israel's priests tried to fill the gap. They'd kill an animal as a sacrifice, but they had to do this every year. It was never enough. Paying indulgences and trying to be a "good person" were just as useless. The Church was still pointing to something even God's law wasn't designed to do.

But God had a plan to redeem us. John Calvin explained it this way:

> [God determined] that the Mediator should be God, and become man. Neither man nor angel, though pure, could have sufficed. The Son of God behooved to come down.[4]

Calvin made an interesting point: Not even the sinless angels could step in and save us. Maybe God could've sent an angel, but He didn't. He decided that we would need a perfect man who would be the necessary mediator and substitute, but also that God Himself would have to do the saving. It couldn't be some ordinary man—it had to be God in the flesh. There would need to be a Second Adam to undo the curse of the first Adam.

How do you and I relate to Adam?

Why is it important to affirm that Jesus is both God and man?

Only God could save us, and only God could step foot on Earth's soil and not be eternally tainted by its brokenness. Those every-year sacrifices pointed to a Man who would not only stand in the gap as a priest, but shed His blood as the sacrifice. Jesus lived the perfect life that Adam (and the rest of us) couldn't live.

GLORY TO GOD ALONE

START

After reflecting on last week's session, name one "savior" you've put in front of the Savior.

In what ways can you put that savior aside and focus on Christ alone?

Have you ever seen a movie that starts at the end? It sounds crazy at first, doesn't it? But sometimes, if you start at the end, it makes the rest of the movie mean more. When you know how it ends, you know how a character's decision is going to impact his or her life. It makes you say, "No! If you do that, you're in trouble!" Or, it makes a particular scene even more epic. It also helps you see how the storyteller is putting everything together.

In the same way, God reveals the end to us. If we flip over to Revelation 22, we get to see the final act of a story that lasts for eternity. This story was written in order for us to worship the Storyteller, to see His glory from start to finish. In the words of John Calvin, the world is God's "theater."[1]

This week, we will see that God's glory affects all the other solas.

THE BIG IDEA

Blessed be the LORD, the God of Israel, who alone does wondrous things. Blessed be his glorious name forever; may the whole earth be filled with his glory! Amen and amen! —*Psalm 72:18-19*

The Bible says that the whole earth is filled with God's glory. But what does that mean? What is God's glory?

In short, God's glory is the total sum of who He is and what He does. It's a powerful force that exudes from His entire being. He is eternal. He is perfect. He is good. He is loving. He is beautiful. He is just. He takes second place to no one. God's glory is the proclamation that He is sovereign over all things, and we see it clearly in creation (He is sovereign, all-powerful, and beautiful) and in salvation (He is loving, just, and merciful).

Luther saw trouble in the Catholic Church because their works-based salvation was stealing glory from God. Since the Church was acting as a filter between people and God, some of His glory was surely getting strained out. More than that, the Church's system was giving people room to boast in their good works and achievements.

Read Psalm 72:18-19 again. List some ways you see God's glory in everyday life.

Looking at your own life, name three ways you intentionally or unintentionally steal glory from God.

GLORY AND HUMILITY IN THE CROSS

It is not sufficient for anyone, and it does him no good to recognize God in his glory and majesty, unless he recognizes him in the humility and shame of the cross. —*Martin Luther*[2]

For Luther and the Reformers, the question was simple: How can anyone recognize God's glory if they don't look at Christ? As Hebrews 1:3 tells us, "He is the radiance of the glory of God and the exact imprint of his nature." If you want to see God's glory, look into the face of Jesus.

According to Luther, to behold the glory of God meant to behold Him crucified on a cross. Just as Christ humbled Himself on the cross, we too must humble ourselves and see the glory of God in a beaten and battered Savior.[3] Pride says we can't worship or see glory in a God who would die, but humility acknowledges that His death brought life. Remember, He didn't stay dead; He walked out of His grave so that we could all one day walk out of ours.

Have you ever thought of Jesus' torture on the cross as glorious? Why or why not?

How His humility glorious? Explain.

JESUS: THE RADIANCE OF GOD'S GLORY

He is the radiance of the glory of God and the exact imprint of his nature. —*Hebrews 1:3*

Jesus is the exact expression—an identical mirror. When you see Him, you see the Father and the glory of God. He was a walking, talking representation of God's glory.

Christians often wish they could just see God in all His glory. We think it might strengthen our belief or help us to worship Him better. But the Israelites showed that this wasn't the case. They saw God's glory on Moses face in Exodus 34 and yet they still struggled with disobedience and doubt throughout their history.

Which describes you most?
[ ] I see God's glory in the good moments in life
[ ] I see God's glory in suffering and frustration

Based on your answer, how can you strike a balance of glorifying God in the good and bad?

THE POWER OF GOD'S GLORY

In the Old Testament, believers could not look directly at God's glory without being changed dramatically. Moses came down the mountain from meeting with God and God's glory shown so bright from Moses face that the others couldn't even look at him (Ex. 34:29). When the prophet Isaiah saw God, he trembled at His majesty (Isa. 6:1-5).

In the New Testament, people were able to see God's glory in the person of Jesus. As truly God in a truly human body, people were able to come close to God's glory rather than be ruined by it. Even in the amazing event called the Transfiguration, in which the glory of God began to shine from Jesus, His disciples were able to see His glory clearly. After witnessing this event and Jesus' life, miracles, death, and resurrection, Peter was able to say, "we were eyewitnesses of his majesty" (2 Pet. 1:16).

Luther wanted people to be witnesses of God's glory for themselves, not through a tinted window provided by the Church's works-based system. The Church was not the keeper of God's glory and the Pope needed to stay away from glorifying his office. God's glory cannot be contained by anyone or anything—not even the Pope and the church.

When you stand next to a plane while its engines are running, you don't just know the engines are on—you feel them. The sheer power of what they are and what they do makes your chest vibrate. In an infinitely more powerful way, God's glory is a soul-vibrating, life-changing force. It's not just a description of who He is and what He does—it's the brilliance of His eternal self. His glory rocks us to the core. And through Scripture and the creation around us, we too are eyewitnesses to His majesty.

We haven't seen Christ physically with our own eyes, but in what ways can we say with Peter that we're "eyewitnesses of his majesty"?

Instead of begging and pleading for God to reveal His glory to us like He did for Moses, Isaiah, or the disciples, let's take to heart what Jesus said about us to His disciples: "Have you believed because you have seen me? Blessed are those who have not seen and yet have believed" (John 20:29). God's glory is readily available to us right now.

All of the echoes of the Reformation find their sound in God's glory. Remember, too, that the Church in Luther's day didn't deny the importance of Scripture, grace, faith, and Christ in salvation. But if you asked about "the little word alone, we would soon find genuine disagreement."[4]

CREATED TO GLORIFY GOD

He has made everything beautiful in its time. Also, he has put eternity into man's heart, yet so that he cannot find out what God has done from the beginning to the end. I perceived that there is nothing better for them than to be joyful and to do good as long as they live; also that everyone should eat and drink and take pleasure in all his toil—this is God's gift to man. I perceived that whatever God does endures forever; nothing can be added to it, nor anything taken from it. God has done it, so that people fear before him. —*Ecclesiastes 3:11-14*

God has "put eternity into man's heart" (v. 11). In other words, whether you recognize it or not, you were created to worship Him. This design is not because He is selfish or lonely, but because the most joyful thing you could ever do is worship God.

Read Ecclesiastes 3:11-14 again. Circle any word in the passage refers to God (including He, Him, etc.).

In what ways does this passage give God glory?

Noticing the number of times God is mentioned and what this passage says about Him, what does this tell us about our own lives?

As Paul told the Corinthians, everything we do is for God's glory (1 Cor. 10:31). Every little thing can glorify God, from enjoying a meal to doing missionary work in China. If our lives were created for God's glory, then nothing we do can be detached from it. Instead, what we do either glorifies Him or doesn't—there's no gray area. But by grace alone, through faith alone, in Christ alone, we are freed to give glory to God alone.

FREE TO WORSHIP

Because Jesus left heaven and came to Earth, because He died on the cross and walked out of the grave, we have been given great freedom. We are released from the power of sin and set free to live for His glory.

When you recognize God's glory, when you become aware that He's been right there the whole time, there's nothing to do but worship Him. His glory shows us that through Jesus, His love is bigger than your sin. He will forgive you every single time. You can lay your life at His feet and say, "It's yours. I'm yours." He won't reject you. He wants to make you whole.

In an average week, how often do you look forward with hope toward the future God has for you?

How can we worship God now, even while still living in a broken world?

FUTURE GLORY

The chief good of man is nothing else but union with God. —*John Calvin*[5]

Last week, we discussed the Reformers' distinction between union with Christ and communion with Christ. Through our union with Christ, God sees us as He sees his Son—perfect and blameless. This is rock solid and unchanging. However, our communion with Christ can change depending on our own hearts. We don't always give our lives to Him like we should.

List three reasons you struggle with communion with God.

In what ways does your union with God help drive your communion with Him?

Will it always be this way? Will we always have a steady union but a shaky communion? The Bible says no. Paul told the Corinthians:

Those whom he foreknew he also predestined to be conformed to the image of his Son, in order that he might be the firstborn among many brothers. And those whom he predestined he also called, and those whom he called he also justified, and those whom he justified he also glorified. —*Romans 8:29-30*

We all, with unveiled face, beholding the glory of the Lord, are being transformed into the same image from one degree of glory to another. For this comes from the Lord who is the Spirit. —*2 Corinthians 3:18*

While there is a lot to say about these passages, let's focus on one major thing: We are being conformed more and more into the image of Christ. And in the image of Christ, we see God's glory (Col. 1:15). So as we become more like Christ—which is what the Holy Spirit is always helping us do—we begin to reflect God's glory. Our character becomes more like God's. Our actions and reactions become more like His.

ALONE MEANS ALONE

> It is that once apparent from the look of their works that they did it all for their own glory, so they were not ashamed to acknowledge and to boast that it was their own glory that they sought. —*Martin Luther*[6]

This was Luther's response to someone saying works played a part in salvation. But if we cannot boast (Eph. 2:8-10), then salvation must be by grace alone, through faith alone, in Christ alone. Anything that involves human effort steals glory from God. Again and again, the Reformers fought for that word *alone* to really mean alone.

Reflecting on what you've read about God's glory so far, list three reasons "God's glory alone" is so crucial to Christian living.

In what ways do you treat the gospel as though it's about your glory instead of God's?

Why is the gospel about God and not us?

GOD'S GLORY TO THE END OF THE EARTH

> Jesus came and said to them, "All authority in heaven and on earth has been given to me. Go therefore and make disciples of all nations, baptizing them in the name of the Father and of the Son and of the Holy Spirit, teaching them to observe all that I have commanded you. And behold, I am with you always, to the end of the age."
> —*Matthew 28:18-20*

We've seen the great commission a few times throughout this study, but we can't see it enough. These were Jesus' final words—the last and perhaps most important thing He said during His rescue mission on Earth. Jesus has authority—ultimate authority—to save people. We go because He has the authority. This means that we can never take credit for our salvation or the salvation of others. God's glory is seen clearly when people worship Him alone.

Back in Genesis 1, the first people received a clear command immediately after they were created. Adam and Eve were given the task to "be fruitful and multiply." This wasn't simply about having children, but about spreading God's image across the globe. He wanted people everywhere glorifying Him. Remember, we are created to glorify God. The more people worship Him, the more His glory is made evident.

Jesus simply tells us to follow the mission our ancient parents were first given—go and make more God-worshipers. Point them to His glory, and let Him do the work. By grace alone, through faith alone, in Christ alone, God alone will get the glory.

If God's glory already fills the world, how does a multitude of people worshiping Him spread His glory across the earth?

Why does God use us to help spread His glory across the globe?

GOSPEL APPLICATION

We live in a man-centered world. All people everywhere, including us, care more about themselves than they care about anyone else. We love and serve ourselves exactly how we want to be loved and served. Maybe that's why Jesus told us to love others like we love ourselves—if we're caring for others the way we care for ourselves, chances are that we'll serve them well. But Jesus didn't want us to be selfish; He wanted us to be sacrificial and think of others first.

Unfortunately, the man-centered world we live in creeps into the church. Sunday mornings are often about what the church can do for us, not what we can do for the church. We want to be "fed" or "encouraged," but we're not as concerned with truly worshiping God or serving others. But Scripture tells us that everything is for God's glory, and nothing else can compare to it.

In what ways is the world man-centered instead of God-centered?

List three people in your life to need to know about God's glory.

We have to remember that the echoes of the Reformation say the same words to us: "*Sola. Sola. Sola. Sola. Sola.*" Five solas. *Alone* on repeat.

We are called not to be man-centered, but to be God-centered. We point away from ourselves. It's not about us. The Church in Luther's day sadly missed this foundational truth, and they began to make salvation about themselves, or at least salvation through themselves.

But going back to Jesus' command to make disciples of all nations, we have to keep the idea of *alone* in mind. We can't preach works-based salvation about getting cleaned up or trying harder. We can't point people to themselves, making salvation about their glory instead of about God's glory. If we tell people that salvation is all about them, then they'll make Christianity man-centered. They'll be right back in the place Luther and the Reformers fought so hard to take us away from.

Telling people about God's glory seems like a daunting task. How can people in a man-centered world respond to a God-centered faith? The same way we all do—by grace alone through faith alone in Christ alone, found in Scripture alone. Remember, salvation is not about us, so saving people isn't about us.

The Holy Spirit was given to us to empower our mission to make disciples of all nations. Even our evangelism is powered by the Holy Spirit, under the authority of Jesus, pointing back to the Father. We are merely the messengers of the greatest news ever told—that God saves sinners, and we don't have to become perfect for Him to do so.

How has this study on the Reformation changed the way you view God and the gospel?

TAKEAWAYS

Over the last few weeks, you've studied a bit of church history as we dug into what the Reformation stood for and what it still stands for today:

Sola Scriptura (By Scripture alone)

Sola gratia (By grace alone)

Sola fide (Through faith alone)

Solus Christus (Through Christ alone)

Soli Deo gloria (Glory to God alone)

We've learned how these five solas, or core truths of our faith, are still vital to our lives. Like Luther decided 500 years ago, will we choose to stand strong in the foundations of our faith, even when the world around us seems set against what we believe? Will we cling tightly to the authority of Scripture, to the truth that salvation only comes by grace through faith in Christ, and to the knowledge that the point of our lives is God's glory?

Reminding ourselves of these core truths points us back to what's important— to the One in whom we find truth, grace, and salvation. And He is the One who deserves all the glory. It is our hope that the solas not remain only a part of our church history, but guide us as we daily live out our faith.

LEADER GUIDE

GETTING STARTED

- Take a few minutes to go around the room. Ask students to introduce themselves and to tell one thing they know about the reformation. This will be a good lead-in to the study and will give you an idea of what students already know.

- Use the "Start" section on page 9 to engage students and get them thinking about the Reformation and how it applies to them today. The correct order to the activity in the "Start" section is:

  » Christopher Columbus discovered America

  » The settlement of Jamestown

  » Establishment of Plymouth Colony

  » Harvard College founded

  » The First Great Awakening

  » Benjamin Franklin's famous kite experiment

  » Boston Tea Party

  » The Declaration of Independence

  » The end of the American Revolutionary War

- Review and discuss "The Big Idea" and "Gospel Application" sections for Session 1. As you lead students through questions addressed in the study, be authentic. Answer the questions truthfully, and share openly with them as you discuss this critical moment in church history and what it means for us today.

HIGHLIGHTS

- The Church had begun selling indulgences, certificates from the Church that guaranteed to reduce the punishment of sins. As Luther saw it, money was also corrupting everyone in power. On top of that, the Church taught that the Pope could receive direct revelation from God—that he had the same power and access to God's will as the Bible. These problems and more pushed Luther to the edge. Like any good leader, he took action. Like any good pastor, he cared for his people. He stepped out when, it seemed that no one else would.

- Luther never received a formal punishment for his battle against the Church, because he fled Wittenberg and disappeared to another town. While in hiding, he most notably translated the entire New Testament into German. In 1521, the Diet of Worms reached a decision, declaring that Luther was a heretic, and that no one should follow his teachings. Unfortunately for the Church—but fortunately for us—his influence couldn't be squashed. The Reformation had begun.

- For Luther and the Reformers, belief in action meant sometimes losing the things they loved. For Luther, it was first his relationship with his father, and later it was his ministry in the Church. For the people in the Bible, belief in action often meant physical or emotional suffering, yet they are our heroes in the faith—and their joy outweighed their grief.

TAKE ACTION

- **Memorize:** Read through Hebrews 12:1-2 as a group. Remind students that this is the Scripture memory passage for the week, and encourage them to commit it to memory. As their leader, it's important to commit to memorizing it with them.

- **Summarize:** Ask students to explain in their own words why church history is important to their lives today.

BEFORE YOU GO

- Encourage students to find another person in the group to be their accountability partner throughout this study. Consider placing students into pairs for this before the first meeting.

- Remind students to complete the "Digging Deeper" section for Session 1 on page 17. As you complete this section on your own time, make sure to mark, highlight, or jot down anything you want to mention to students in your next meeting.

- Take a few minutes to go around the room and ask students to share any prayer requests they might have. Then, ask for a volunteer to close the group time in prayer.

SESSION 2

GETTING STARTED

- Begin Session 2 by spending a few minutes reviewing and discussing the "Digging Deeper" section from Session 1. Allow enough time for discussion and answering any questions students might have.

- Use the "Start" section on page 19 to begin the session by introducing the first of our five solas—Scripture Alone. This activity will help students see how the first sola applies to them today, as you lead them to understand their need for Scripture as the ultimate authority in their lives.

- Lead students through the "The Big Idea" and "Gospel Application" sections for Session 2. As you lead students through questions in the study, be sure to participate yourself, creating an open environment where questions can be honestly addressed.

HIGHLIGHTS

- Luther didn't view Scripture's authority as a piece of the Christian puzzle, or an important but not ultimate doctrine; it was the concrete slab on which the Christian house stood. For him, the preacher's primary task was to preach God's Word rightly because of its sheer power and unchangeable truth. So, when the Pope exercised authority apart from Scripture or in contradiction to Scripture, Luther would have none of it. Scripture *plus* anything else *equals* truth mixed with error.

- The Reformation caused a massive split in the global Church. Protestants (literally, the protesters) were born. Protestants are a people of the Bible first and foremost. It's in the Bible that we find who God is and how He relates to his people. Following in the footsteps of Luther, Protestants believe that when Scripture speaks, God speaks.

- God's Word is alive. The Bible is not some outdated, crusty book that fits better on a shelf than in our laps. No, it sits there rumbling like an earthquake, holding in the life-changing words of the God of the Universe. It is applicable to your life now—today—and for all eternity. If we believe that Scripture truly is the Word of God, we will believe what it says. Like Luther, we will believe that a doctrine is true only if it's found in the Bible. There are many important truths we can learn from the reformation, but the most important is this: We should first take a look at reforming our hearts. We must be open to growing before we can actually grow.

- If we believe that Scripture truly is the Word of God, we will believe what it says. Like Luther, we will believe that a doctrine is true only if it's found in the Bible.

- The Word does it all. Saying that Scripture alone is our final authority is not a cop out—it's confidence. Because of sin, we are fragile people. We can't save anyone. We can't "be Jesus" to anyone. Oh, but we can point them to the beauty of God's Word and to the story of the life, death, and resurrection of Christ found in its pages. We aren't confident in ourselves, but we are supremely confident in God and the power of His Word.

TAKE ACTION

- **Memorize:** Find a volunteer to read 2 Timothy 3:16-17 aloud. Remind students that this is the Scripture memory passage for the week, and encourage them to commit it to memory. As their leader, it's important to commit to memorizing it with them.

- **Summarize:** Ask students to explain in their own words the Reformational belief in "Scripture Alone" and why it's important for their lives today.

BEFORE YOU GO

- Remind students to complete the "Digging Deeper" section for Session 2 on pages 26-27. As you complete this section on your own time, make sure to mark, highlight, or jot down anything you want to mention to students in your next meeting.

- As you close your group time, pray over the group. Ask God to help students to remember to seek Him first, recognizing Him and His Word as the ultimate authority in their lives.

- Encourage students to continue to meet with their accountability partners to talk through what they've learned each week.

GETTING STARTED

- Begin Session 3 by spending a few minutes reviewing and discussing the "Digging Deeper" section from Session 2. Allow enough time for discussion and answering any questions students might have.

- Use the "Start" section on page 29 to begin the session by introducing our second sola—"Grace Alone." This activity will help students see how the second sola applies to them today, as you lead them to understand that no amount of works can achieve right standing before God—only *by* the gift of His grace and through faith in Christ are we saved.

- Lead students through the "The Big Idea" and "Gospel Application" sections for Session 3. As you lead students through questions in the study, be sure to participate yourself, creating an open environment where questions can be honestly addressed.

HIGHLIGHTS

- The Catholic Church was trying to sell grace to people. Through indulgences and other goods, they were packaging up grace with a nice bow on top, creating a sort of Catholic supermarket for God's grace. Luther knew he needed grace, and he also knew that grace came only from God.

- The conflict in our hearts between God and others can't be swept under the rug by a few dollars and an "I'm sorry." It can't be done by just working hard. We don't bring anything to the table. We are loved and cherished by God as special creatures made in His image, but this doesn't mean we are perfect or without sin. A life of repentance—of continually turning from our sin and turning to Jesus—is the byproduct of grace, not the cause of it. No one is righteous (Rom. 3:10). That's why we need the Righteous One. Repentance, then, must be something we do often. We should constantly push away sin and pull closer to Christ.

- Looking back at Jesus' ministry, He made a point of telling people He was the only way to God (John 14:6). Jesus even rebuked the religious leaders of His day for thinking salvation could be found in their own worthiness or works and for teaching people to live up to impossible religious standards (Matt. 23:13-39). As Luther recognized, Jesus' teaching and the Church's teaching didn't match up.

- Our identity is more than our accomplishments, goals, and good morals. It's also more than our sins, struggles, and situations. The gospel tells us that even on our best days, we still needed Jesus to die on the cross for our sins. The gospel also tells us that on our worst days, Jesus loved us enough to die for us. Whether you are puffed up with pride or beaten down by frustration, the gospel has something to say to you—you're not as good as you think you are, and you're not as hopeless as you think you are.

TAKE ACTION

- **Memorize:** Read through Romans 3:23-24 as a group. Remind students that this is the Scripture memory passage for the week, and encourage them to commit it to memory. As their leader, it's important to commit to memorizing it with them.

- **Summarize:** Ask students to explain in their own words the Reformational belief in "Grace Alone" and why it's important for their lives today.

BEFORE YOU GO

- Remind students to complete the "Digging Deeper" section for Session 3 on pages 36-37. As you complete this section on your own time, make sure to mark, highlight, or jot down anything you want to mention to students in your next meeting.

- Close the group time in prayer. Throughout the week, commit to praying for students to develop a deeper understanding of what "Grace Alone" truly means.

- Encourage students to continue to meet with their accountability partners to talk through what they've learned each week.

GETTING STARTED

- Begin Session 4 by spending a few minutes reviewing and discussing the "Digging Deeper" section from Session 3. Allow enough time for discussion and answering any questions students might have.

- Use the "Start" section on page 39 to begin the session. Provide a bandanna and prepare an obstacle course ahead of time, then follow the instructions on page 39 as you lead students through the activity.

- Introduce the third sola—"Faith Alone." The obstacle course activity will help students see how the third sola applies to them today, as you lead them to understand how only by grace, *through* faith in Jesus Christ are we able to be saved.

- Lead students through the "The Big Idea" and "Gospel Application" sections for Session 4. As you lead students through questions in the study, be sure to participate yourself, creating an open environment where questions can be honestly addressed.

HIGHLIGHTS

- The world continually tells us that we can justify ourselves. We can be good people if we just become better students, better friends, or better sons, daughters, brothers, and sisters. The world tells us if we're simply kind enough to others, then surely God won't judge us. But that's not true. Without Christ, God will surely judge us. Even spiritually dead people can be good neighbors, but that doesn't save anyone. We need more. We need Jesus' life, death, burial, and resurrection because He is the way to salvation (John 14:6). We need to be constantly reminded that when God looks at His sinful people, He sees the perfect righteousness of His Son. That's the only hope we have.

- Salvation is God's gift to us, which means that faith and grace are both gifts. If God wanted to deny us faith, or even the ability to have faith, He could. But because of His fierce love for us, He graciously provided a way for us through faith in His Son. We were dead in our sins, but by grace through faith, we are made alive in Christ (Eph. 2:1-7).

- Every year, the high priest in Israel would enter the tabernacle and kill an animal, whose blood would cover the sins of the people. Every year another animal, another pool of blood. This was non-stop, year in and year out for the people of Israel. However, the writer of Hebrews gives us the good news: Christ doesn't have to climb back up on the cross every year. He is the High Priest who *made* the sacrifice and *was* the sacrifice. He shed his blood once, for all of us. Jesus Christ was able to make the perfect sacrifice because He was a sinless man and a spotless lamb (1 Pet. 1:19). None of us can be Jesus, and God doesn't expect us to. We should only expect that Christ's righteousness has been imputed to us, by grace alone through faith alone. As Luther taught, righteousness is not something we have—it is a gift we receive.

- The Bible teaches us that sin brings death and we can't save ourselves by our own works. If that's true (and it is), it's easy to see why faith alone is important. If you don't understand salvation by grace alone through faith alone, you'll keep trying to save yourself—and you'll fail. Your own attempts at salvation don't lead to eternal life, but to eternal death.

TAKE ACTION

- **Memorize:** Find a volunteer to read Ephesians 2:8-9. Remind students that this is the Scripture memory passage for the week, and encourage them to commit it to memory. As their leader, it's important to commit to memorizing it with them.

- **Summarize:** Ask students to explain in their own words the Reformational belief in "Faith Alone" and why it's important for their lives today.

BEFORE YOU GO

- Remind students to complete the "Digging Deeper" section for Session 4 on pages 46-47. As you complete this section on your own time, make sure to mark, highlight, or jot down anything you want to mention to students in your next meeting.

- Take a few minutes to go around the room and ask students to share any prayer requests they might have. Then, ask for a volunteer to close the group time in prayer. Throughout the week, pray that they would grow in their understanding of "Faith Alone."

- Encourage students to continue to meet with their accountability partners to talk through what they've learned each week.

SESSION 5

GETTING STARTED

- Begin Session 5 by spending a few minutes reviewing and discussing the "Digging Deeper" section from Session 4. Allow enough time for discussion and answering any questions students might have.

- Use the "Start" section on page 49 to begin the session by introducing the fourth sola—"Christ Alone." This activity will help students see how the fourth sola applies to them today, as you lead them to understand that only Christ provides all that we need for salvation.

- Lead students through the "The Big Idea" and "Gospel Application" sections for Session 5. As you lead students through questions in the study, be sure to participate yourself, creating an open environment where questions can be honestly addressed.

HIGHLIGHTS

- Before sin entered the world, mankind was perfect. Adam and Eve lived in perfect harmony with God and with each other. But as Paul tells us, Adam brought sin and death into the world (Rom. 5:17). Now we all, from the beginning, inherit a sinful nature from our first father. One sin brought death and destruction into the world. One sin was all it took to separate God from His people, because sin cannot dwell with God—not even one.

- In order to bring us back to God, there had to be a man who could be a mediator—a go-between—that could bridge the gap between God and His people. Israel's priests tried to fill the gap. They killed an animal as a sacrifice, but they had to do this every year—it was never enough. Paying indulgences and trying to be a "good person" were just as useless. The Church was still pointing to something even God's law wasn't designed to do.

- Christ alone can save us. No imitation saviors will do the trick. Neither will gathering up indulgences or begging priests for their special prayers. When the Church told people that buying indulgences and confessing sins to the priests contributed to salvation, they were putting other saviors next to the Savior. The Church wasn't about Scripture alone, grace alone, or faith alone—and it certainly wasn't about Christ alone, because all of those things flow from Him.

- It's important to understand that our union with Christ is tied directly to the Father. So when we say, "When God looks at us, He doesn't see our sin; instead, He sees Jesus' righteousness," we are talking about our union with Christ. When Paul told the Galatians, "I have been crucified with Christ," he was talking about his union with Christ. We are so united with Christ that we might as well have been on the cross with Him. Remember, God didn't wave a magic wand and erase all our sins. Instead, God in the flesh lived a real human life and died a real human death. He lived a life we couldn't, but that doesn't mean our lives are disconnected from His.

TAKE ACTION

- **Memorize:** Read through John 14:6-7 as a group. Remind students that this is the Scripture memory passage for the week, and encourage them to commit it to memory. As their leader, it's important to commit to memorizing it with them.

- **Summarize:** Ask students to explain in their own words the Reformational belief in "Christ Alone" and why it's important for their lives today.

BEFORE YOU GO

- Remind students to complete the "Digging Deeper" section for Session 5 on pages 56-57. As you complete this section on your own time, make sure to mark, highlight, or jot down anything you want to mention to students in your next meeting.

- As you close your group time, pray over the group. Ask God to help students understand what it means that only Jesus Christ could be the perfect, once for all sacrifice and provide the only way to be made right with God.

- Encourage students to continue to meet with their accountability partners to talk through what they've learned each week.

GETTING STARTED

- Begin Session 6 by spending a few minutes reviewing and discussing the "Digging Deeper" section from Session 5. Allow enough time for discussion and answering any questions students might have.

- Use the "Start" section on page 59 to begin the session by introducing the fifth and final sola—"to God's Glory Alone." This activity will help students see how the final sola applies to them today, as you lead them to understand how this sola affects all of the other solas and influences every area of life.

- Lead students through the "The Big Idea" and "Gospel Application" sections for Session 6. As you lead students through questions in the study, be sure to participate yourself, creating an open environment where questions can be honestly addressed.

HIGHLIGHTS

- Since no one else is God, no one else can share His glory (Isa. 48:11). Being prideful about our own efforts and good deeds is glory-stealing. Further, the humility of God Himself hanging on the cross erases any shred of pride we have left.

- Jesus Himself was clear about His relationship with His Father throughout His ministry. For example, He often said things like, "If you had known me, you would have known my Father also" (John 14:7) and, "Whatever you ask in my name, this I will do, that the Father may be glorified in the Son" (John 14:13). In other words, if you want to see God's glory, look at the face of Jesus. Think about it: If God's glory is who He is and what He does, and Jesus is God in the flesh, then of course we see God's glory when we see Jesus. God's glory is seen in Jesus' holiness, perfection, love, kindness, and so much more. Who was more holy, perfect, loving, kind, and so on, than Jesus Christ?

- The Book of Revelation tells us that God will make all things new in the end. Everything that is broken will become unbroken. One day, no one will be blind to His glory. Everyone will see it. God tells us that His glory will be so bright, so clear, that we won't need the sun anymore (Rev. 22:5)! You can read this in the Bible right now. You can see the final scene. And because you've seen the end already, you know that things will work out for good. You know that your life is not a waste, and that the story is about the glory of God, not about how many times you've fallen down.

- If our glory days truly are ahead, it'll only be through our union with Christ. After all, we spend eternity with God in that glorious future only because of grace alone, through faith alone, in Christ alone. Our future is grounded in that union. But the way we glorify God is through our communion with Him—we can't worship Him in all His glory if we're ignoring His glory.

TAKE ACTION

- **Memorize:** Find a volunteer to read Psalm 72:18-19. Remind students that this is the Scripture memory passage for the week, and encourage them to commit it to memory. As their leader, it's important to commit to memorizing it with them.

- **Summarize:** Ask students to explain in their own words the Reformational belief in "God's Glory Alone" and why it's important for their lives today.

BEFORE YOU GO

- Since this is the last session, wrap up your group time by clarifying any questions students may have about the solas or their importance to us today.

- Close the group time in prayer. Commit to praying for students to develop a deeper understanding of what "to God's Glory Alone" truly means. Ask God to guide students as they apply what they've learned in this study.

- Encourage students to continue to meet with their accountability partners to talk through what they've learned throughout their study of the Reformation.

TIPS FOR LEADING A SMALL GROUP

PRAYERFULLY PREPARE

Prepare for each group session with prayer. Ask the Holy Spirit to work through you and the group discussion as you point to Jesus each week through God's Word.

REVIEW the weekly material and group questions ahead of time.

PRAY for each person in the group.

MINIMIZE DISTRACTIONS

Do everything in your ability to help students focus on what's most important: connecting with God, with the Bible, and with one another.

CREATE A COMFORTABLE ENVIRONMENT. If students are uncomfortable, they'll be distracted and therefore not engaged in the group experience.

TAKE INTO CONSIDERATION seating, temperature, lighting, refreshments, surrounding noise, and general cleanliness.

Thoughtfulness and hospitality show guests and group members they're welcome and valued in whatever environment you choose to gather.

INCLUDE OTHERS

Your goal is to foster a community in which people are welcome just as they are but encouraged to grow spiritually. Always be aware of opportunities to include and invite.

INCLUDE anyone who visits the group.

INVITE new people to join your group.

ENCOURAGE DISCUSSION

A good small-group experience has the following characteristics.

EVERYONE PARTICIPATES. Encourage everyone to ask questions, share responses, or read aloud.

NO ONE DOMINATES—NOT EVEN THE LEADER. Be sure your time speaking as a leader takes up less than half your time together as a group. Politely guide discussion if anyone dominates.

NOBODY IS RUSHED THROUGH QUESTIONS. Don't feel that a moment of silence is a bad thing. People often need time to think about their responses to questions they've just heard or to gain courage to share what God is stirring in their hearts.

INPUT IS AFFIRMED AND FOLLOWED UP. Make sure you point out something true or helpful in a response. Don't just move on. Build community with follow-up questions, asking how other students have experienced similar things or how a truth has shaped their understanding of God and the Scripture you're studying. Students are less likely to speak up if they fear that you don't actually want to hear their answers or that you're looking for only a certain answer.

GOD AND HIS WORD ARE CENTRAL. Opinions and experiences can be helpful, but God has given us the truth. Trust Scripture to be the authority and God's Spirit to work in students' lives. You can't change anyone, but God can. Continually point students to the Word and to active steps of faith.

KEEP CONNECTING

Think of ways to connect with students during the week. Participation during the group session is always improved when students spend time connecting with one another outside the group sessions. The more people are comfortable with and involved in one another's lives, the more they'll look forward to being together. When students move beyond being friendly to truly being friends who form a community, they come to each session eager to engage instead of merely attending.

ENCOURAGE STUDENTS with thoughts, commitments, or questions from the session by connecting through emails, texts, and social media.

BUILD DEEPER FRIENDSHIPS by planning or spontaneously inviting students to join you outside your regularly scheduled group time for meals; fun activities; and projects around your home, church, or community.

SOURCES

SESSION 1

1. Justo L. Gonzalez, *The Story of Christianity, Vol. 1: The Early Church and the Dawn of the Reformation* (New York: HarperCollins, 2010), 3.

2. Martin Luther, as quoted in Stephen J. Nichols, *The Reformation: How a Monk and a Mallet Changed the World* (Wheaton: Crossway, 2007), 37.

3. Martin Luther, as quoted Roland H. Bainton, *Here I Stand: A Life of Martin Luther* (Nashville: Abingdon Press, 1978), 25.

4. Carl R. Trueman, *Luther on the Christian Life: Cross and Freedom* (Wheaton: Crossway, 2015), 38.

5. Martin Luther, as quoted in *Documents from the History of Lutheranism, 1517–1750,* ed. Eric Lund (Minneapolis: Fortress, 2002), 32.

6. John Calvin, as quoted in Timothy George, *Theology of the Reformers*, rev. ed. (Nashville: Broadman & Holman, 2013), 242.

SESSION 2

1. Martin Luther quoted in Timothy George, *Theology of the Reformers*, rev. ed. (Nashville: Broadman & Holman, 2013), 81.

2. Martin Luther, as quoted in *Documents from the History of Lutheranism, 1517–1750*, ed. Eric Lund (Minneapolis: Fortress, 2002), 32.

3. Martin Luther, *Martin Luther's Ninety-Five Theses and Selected Sermons* (Radford: Wilder Publications, 2008), 50.

4. Barna Group, "The State of the Bible," *American Bible Society*, accessed July 13, 2016, available online at http://www.americanbible.org/uploads/content/state-of-the-bible-data-analysis-american-bible-society-2014.pdf.

5. Martin Luther, as quoted in George, *Theology of the Reformers*, 104.

6. Charles Partee, *The Theology of John Calvin* (Louisville: Westminster John Knox Press, 2008), 68.

7. Martin Luther, as quoted in George, *Theology of the Reformers*, 54.

SESSION 3

1. Carl R. Trueman, *Luther on the Christian Life: Cross and Freedom* (Wheaton: Crossway, 2015), 54.

2. Michael Reeves and Tim Chester, *Why the Reformation Still Matters* (Wheaton: Crossway, 2016), 81.

3. Martin Luther, as quoted in Reeves and Chester, *Why the Reformation Still Matters*, 84.

4. Huldrych Zwingli, as quoted in Michael Reeves and Tim Chester, *Why the Reformation Still Matters*, 49.

5. John Calvin, *St. Paul's Epistles to Timothy, Titus and Philemon*, The John Calvin Bible Commentaries (Altenmünster, Germany: Jazzybee Verlag, n.d.).

SESSION 4

1. Martin Luther, *A Commentary on St. Paul's Epistle to the Galatians* (London: James Duncan, 1830), 75.

2. Herman J. Selderhuis, *Calvin's Theology of the Psalms*, (Grand Rapids: Baker Academic, 2007), 270, quoted in Michael Horton, *Calvin on the Christian Life: Glorifying and Enjoying God Forever* (Wheaton: Crossway, 2014), 97.

3. Michael Horton, *Calvin on the Christian Life: Glorifying and Enjoying God Forever* (Wheaton: Crossway, 2014), 127.

4. Martin Luther, as quoted in Timothy George, *Theology of the Reformers*, rev. ed. (Nashville: Broadman & Holman, 2013), 69.

SESSION 5

1. Martin Luther, as quoted in Timothy J. Wengert, *Martin Luther's Ninety-Five Theses: With Introduction, Commentary, and Study Guide* (Minneapolis: Fortress Press, 2015), 18-19.

2. Huldrych Zwingli, as quoted in Timothy George, *Theology of the Reformers*, rev. ed. (Nashville: Broadman & Holman, 2013), 129.

3. Martin Luther, as quoted in Michael Reeves and Tim Chester, *Why the Reformation Still Matters* (Wheaton: Crossway, 2016), 122.

4. John Calvin, *Institutes of the Christian Religion*, trans. Henry Beveridge (Peabody: Hendrickson Publishers, 2008), 297.

SESSION 6

1. John Calvin, *Institutes of the Christian Religion*, trans. Henry Beveridge (Peabody: Hendrickson Publishers, 2008), 27.

2. Martin Luther, as quoted in David VanDrunen, *God's Glory Alone: The Majestic Heart of Christian Faith and Life* (Grand Rapids: Zondervan, 2015), 13.

3. VanDrunen, *God's Glory Alone*, 13.

4. VanDrunen, *God's Glory Alone*, 14.

5. John Calvin, as quoted in Michael Reeves and Tim Chester, *Why the Reformation Still Matters* (Wheaton: Crossway, 2016), 211.

6. Martin Luther, *The Bondage of the Will*, trans. J. I. Packer and O. R. Johnson (Grand Rapids: Revell, 1957), 251-52.

NOTES

NOTES

NOTES

NOTES

NOTES

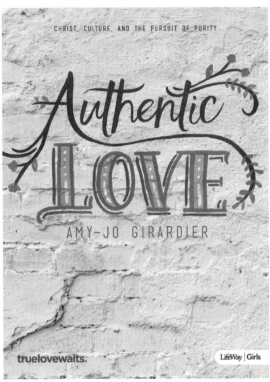